Table of Contents

I

Executive Summary

Over the past two decades, the Internet has become increasingly important to the nation's economic competitiveness, to promoting innovation, and to our collective well-being. As the Internet continues to grow in all aspects of our lives, there is emerging a parallel, ongoing increase and evolution in, and emergence of, cybersecurity risks.

Today's cybersecurity threats include indiscriminate and broad-based attacks designed to exploit the interconnectedness of the Internet. Increasingly, they also involve targeted attacks, the purpose of which is to steal, manipulate, destroy or deny access to sensitive data, or to disrupt computing systems. These threats are exacerbated by the interconnected and interdependent architecture of today's computing environment. Theoretically, security deficiencies in one area may provide opportunities for exploitations elsewhere.

Despite increasing awareness of the associated risks, broad swaths of the economy and individual actors, ranging from consumers to large businesses, still do not take advantage of available technology and processes to secure their systems, nor are protective measures evolving as quickly as the threats. This general lack of investment puts firms and consumers at greater risk, leading to economic loss at the individual and aggregate level and poses a threat to national security.

President Obama's *Cyberspace Policy Review* in May 2009 articulated the many reasons government must work closely with the private sector and other partners to address these risks. As stated in the *Review*, "[i]nformation and communications networks are largely owned and operated by the private sector, both nationally and internationally. Thus, addressing network security issues requires a public-private partnership as well as international cooperation and norms."

In addition, the Administration has promoted cybersecurity legislation that would catalyze the development of norms for practices of entities that maintain our critical infrastructure. These entities include sectors such as energy, critical manufacturing and emergency services whose disruption would have a debilitating impact on individual security, national economic security, national public health and safety. The proposed legislation requires these entities to a develop baseline framework of protection based on risk – a function of threat, vulnerability, and consequences. The Department of Homeland Security (DHS), in coordination with sector-specific agencies and other relevant departments, would promulgate the list of covered entities using the established criteria and input from the federal government, state and local governments, and the private sector.

The U.S. Department of Commerce has focused its efforts on developing public policies and private sector norms whose voluntary adoption could improve the overall cybersecurity posture of private sector infrastructure operators, software and service providers, and users outside the critical infrastructure. Entities in these areas have not been the main focus of cybersecurity activities to date, yet they can be at great risk – and can put others at great risk – if they do not adequately secure their networks and services. Yet, attempting to develop policy to protect each industry, regardless of criticality, with equal weight will lead to placing too much emphasis on lesser concerns. We must instead find the right protections for each sector and sub-sector and promote the right policies to get them implemented.

In early 2010, the Department of Commerce launched an Internet Policy Task Force (Task Force), charged with addressing the Internet's most pressing policy issues and with recommending new policies. After several months of consultations with stakeholders, the Task Force published a Notice of Inquiry (NOI) and convened a symposium on Cybersecurity, Innovation, and the Internet Economy leading to this preliminary set of recommendations in the Green Paper. In this paper, the Task Force asks many follow up questions to gain additional feedback and to help the Department of Commerce determine how to proceed. The goal of this undertaking is to ensure that the Task Force is on the right course in our recommendations and to identify technical and policy measures that might close the gap between today's status quo and reasonably achievable levels of cyber-protection outside of critical infrastructure sectors.

In particular, many responses to the NOI highlighted a large group of functions and services that should be the subject of our efforts. The Task Force is calling this group the "Internet and Information Innovation Sector" (I3S). The I3S includes functions and services that create or utilize the Internet or networking services and have large potential for growth, entrepreneurship, and vitalization of the economy, but would fall outside the classification of covered critical infrastructure as defined by existing law and Administration policy. Business models may differ, but the following functions and services are included in the I3S:

- provision of information services and content;
- facilitation of the wide variety of transactional services available through the Internet as an intermediary;
- storage and hosting of publicly accessible content; and

- support of users' access to content or transaction activities, including, but not limited to application, browser, social network, and search providers.

The I3S is comprised of companies, from small business to "brick and mortar-based firms" with online services to large companies that only exist on the Internet, that are significantly impacted by cybersecurity concerns, yet do not have the same level of operational criticality that would cause them to be designated as covered critical infrastructure. The Task Force supports efforts to increase the security posture of I3S services and functions from cybersecurity risks without regulating these services as covered critical infrastructure. A primary goal of this Green Paper is to spark a discussion of the scope of this new sector and the policies needed to protect it independently of, but in concert with, the discussion on protections within the critical infrastructure.

Based on the record from the NOI, the Task Force makes the following preliminary recommendations and identifies several areas where it seeks additional public input. Our recommendations and follow-up questions fall into four broad categories. Specifically:

1. **Create a nationally recognized approach to minimize vulnerabilities for the I3S**

   The Department of Commerce should work with multi-stakeholder groups to develop, when necessary, nationally recognized, consensus-based standards and practices for the I3S. These should be applicable to entities of different sizes and types to facilitate implementation and minimize risk profiles. The multi-stakeholder process should rely on the expertise of industry, academic, consumer and public interest groups, and federal, state and local government.

   a. **Facilitate the development of I3S- specific, consensus-based codes of conduct**: The rapid development and implementation of sector-specific, consensus-based codes of conduct is critical to protecting the I3S from cybersecurity threats. The Department of Commerce can play an important role to convene the I3S and related sectors and industries and facilitate their development of voluntary codes of conduct. Where sectors (such as those with a large number of small businesses) lack the capacity to establish their own voluntary codes of conduct, new and existing National Institute of Standards Technology (NIST) guidelines would be available to bridge gaps in security protection.

b. **Promote adoption of particular keystone standards and practices**: Given the constant evolution of cyber threats, the most immediate impact the federal government can have in promoting security within the I3S and beyond is by encouraging the market to provide competitive and innovative technology solutions. Where consensus emerges that a particular standard or practice will markedly improve the Nation's collective security, the government should consider more proactively promoting their implementation and use. The Department of Commerce plans to better promote these efforts as a starting point to building better general industry practices.

c. **Accelerate promotion of automation in security**: As codes of conduct are created and implemented, and as there is greater reliance on emerging technologies such as cloud computing, increasing the ability to better automate security and compliance becomes an ever-important ingredient in strong security practices. Work to research and develop automated security should accelerate.

d. **Improve and modernize security assurance**: The federal government should work with the private sector to step-up the pace of its efforts to improve and augment security assurance. One such effort is the "Common Criteria,"[1] which are used to assess the security of products purchased by government agencies. While the Common Criteria offer a starting point, they are insufficiently flexible for a rapidly changing marketplace. Efforts to improve assurance models in the private sector and among government agencies are important for the future of security efforts. If the government wants private actors to develop and maintain codes of conduct that evolve more rapidly, it should lead by example.

2. Develop incentives for I3S to combat cybersecurity threats

The Department of Commerce should work with industry to create, through public policy and public/private partnerships and other means, new incentives for firms to follow nationally-recognized standards and practices as consensus around them emerges.

---

[1] The "Common Criteria" refers to the International Common Criteria for Information Technology Security Evaluation, which is an international standard (ISO/IEC 15408).

a. **Using security disclosure as an incentive**: The Task Force already has endorsed the creation of a national cyber-breach notification law, in part, because requiring such disclosures may encourage firms to take more care to avoid breaches in the first place.

b. **Facilitate information sharing and other public/private partnerships in the I3S to improve cybersecurity**: More expansive sharing of information regarding cyber incidents would not only encourage broader adoption of consensus practices, but also increase defensive knowledge. Involvement of appropriate federal and state agencies and/or relevant public/private partnerships will be key to coordinating successfully with the I3S.

c. **Develop the right mix of incentives to promote adoption of cybersecurity best practices**: There are a number of public policy tools (including liability protection, insurance models, and others) available to provide the incentives for I3S to adopt cybersecurity best practices. However, we know that to date some within the I3S have been slow to adopt protective technologies and best practices that are responsive to new threats as they emerge. We need to develop the correct incentives to ingrain these best practices into the culture of firms of all sizes and minimize the need for greater regulation on the I3S in the future.

3. Education and Research

The Department of Commerce should work with the I3S and other federal agencies to deepen private sector and public understanding of cybersecurity vulnerabilities, threats, and responses in order to improve incentives, R&D, and education.

a. **Develop better cost/benefit analysis for I3S cybersecurity**: A stronger understanding (at both the firm and at the macro-economic level) of the costs of cyber-incidents and the benefits of greater security.

b. **Measure I3S cybersecurity education efforts**: Better targeting and tailoring of future awareness-raising efforts should build on measurement of current education efforts including the awareness, education, and training done through the National Initiative for Cybersecurity Education (NICE).

c. **Facilitate research and development for deployable technologies**: A greater focus on technologies that can aid I3S entities in the near future is essential to help address the growing demand for efficient and effective technological solutions.

4. International Cooperation

The Department of Commerce should continue and enhance its international collaboration and cooperation activities to promote shared research and development goals, enable sharing of best practices and threat information, and promote cybersecurity standards and policies that are in line with and/or influence global practices. Such activities will help build continued innovation and enable economic growth for the United States and globally.

I. Introduction

A.   *Cybersecurity Today*

The Internet allows users to gather, store, process, and transfer vast amounts of data, including proprietary and sensitive business, transactional, and personal data. At the same time that businesses and consumers rely more and more on such capabilities, cybersecurity threats continue to plague the Internet economy. Cybersecurity threats evolve as rapidly as the Internet expands, and the associated risks are becoming increasingly global. Staying protected against cybersecurity threats requires all users, even the most sophisticated ones, to be aware of the threats and improve their security practices on an ongoing basis. Creating incentives to motivate all parties in the Internet economy to make appropriate security investments requires technical and public policy measures that are carefully balanced to heighten cybersecurity without creating barriers to innovation, economic growth, and the free flow of information.

Concern over the proliferation of cybersecurity threats is well-documented and well-founded.[2] The May 2009 report to the President, "Cyberspace Policy Review: Assuring a Trusted and Resilient Information and Communications Infrastructure," made clear that maintaining an Internet "environment that promotes efficiency, innovation, economic prosperity, and free trade while also promoting safety, security, civil liberties, and privacy rights" must be a top priority for the nation.[3] Yet, reaching this goal is not an easy task. The constantly evolving nature of threats and vulnerabilities not only affects individual firms and their customers, but collectively the threats pose a persistent economic and national security challenge. As the Review made clear, sharing responsibility to protect cybersecurity across all relevant sectors is becoming ever more important. Computing devices are highly and increasingly interconnected, which means security deficiencies in a limited number of systems can be exploited to launch cyber intrusions or attacks on other systems. Stated another way, poor cyber "hygiene" on one Internet-connected computer negatively impacts other connected computers.

---

[2] *See, e.g.*, Center for Strategic and International Studies, *Significant Cyber Incidents Since 2006* (2010), *available at* http://csis.org/files/publication/110309_Significant_Cyber_Incidents_Since_2006.pdf.

[3] THE WHITE HOUSE, CYBERSPACE POLICY REVIEW: ASSURING A TRUSTED AND RESILIENT INFORMATION AND COMMUNICATIONS INFRASTRUCTURE 5 (2009) [hereinafter CYBERSPACE POLICY REVIEW], *available at* http://www.whitehouse.gov/assets/documents/Cyberspace_Policy_Review_final.pdf.

Given the breadth and importance of this challenge, government and private sector actors have pursued a range of mitigation strategies over the years. Currently at the federal level, the White House's Cybersecurity Coordinator is responsible for setting a national agenda and for coordinating Executive Branch cybersecurity activities.[4] Specific federal activities in this area include research and training, threat reporting and analysis, information collection and dissemination, consumer awareness, and policy development.[5] DHS plays a central role in the U.S. government's efforts to secure cyberspace working with public and private stakeholders to protect critical infrastructure[6] and key resources[7] (CIKR).

The Department of Commerce has many cybersecurity programs that complement other federal and private sector efforts. NIST develops standards and guides for securing non-national security federal information systems. It works with industry and other agencies to define minimum-security requirements for federally held information and for information systems that are often important in the private sector, both for CIKR and non-critical infrastructure as well. NIST identifies methods and metrics for assessing the effectiveness of security requirements; evaluates private sector security policies for potential federal agency use; and provides general cybersecurity technical support and assistance to the private sector and federal agencies. Moreover, over the past two decades, the Department of Commerce's National Telecommunications and Information Administration (NTIA), in its role as principal adviser to the President on telecommunications and information policies, has worked closely with other parts of government on broadband deployment, Internet policy development, securing the Internet domain name space, and other issues. As an advocate for electronic commerce, NTIA has played an instrumental role in developing policies that have helped commerce over the Internet flourish.

---

[4] *Id.* at 7-9; *see also* THE WHITE HOUSE, THE COMPREHENSIVE NATIONAL CYBERSECURITY INITIATIVE 1 (2009) [hereinafter CYBERSECURITY INITIATIVE], *available at* http://www.whitehouse.gov/sites/default/files/cybersecurity.pdf ("In May 2009, the President accepted the recommendations of the [] Cyberspace Policy Review, including the selection of an Executive Branch Cybersecurity Coordinator . . . .").

[5] *See generally* CYBERSECURITY INITIATIVE, *supra* note 4, at 1-5.

[6] Part of the USA PATRIOT Act, the Critical Infrastructures Protection Act of 2001, 42 U.S.C. § 5195c(e) (2006), defines the term "critical infrastructure" to mean "systems and assets, whether physical or virtual, so vital to the United States that the incapacity or destruction of such systems and assets would have a debilitating impact on security, national economic security, national public health or safety, or any combination of those matters."

[7] Homeland Security Act of 2002, 6 U.S.C. § 101(10) (2006) ("The term 'key resources' means publicly or privately controlled resources essential to the minimal operations of the economy and government.").

Through its Task Force, the Department of Commerce will recommend public policies and promote private sector norms aimed at markedly improving the overall cybersecurity posture of private sector infrastructure operators, software and service providers, and users outside the critical infrastructure and key resources realm and of their customers.

The Department of Commerce NOI aimed to identify public policies and private-sector norms that can: (1) promote conduct by firms and consumers that collectively sustain growth in the Internet economy and improve the level of security of the infrastructure and online environment that support it; (2) enhance individual and collaborative efforts by those actors who are in the best position to assist firms and their customers in addressing cybersecurity challenges; (3) improve the ability of firms and consumers to keep pace with ever-evolving cybersecurity threats; and (4) promote individual privacy and civil liberties. The NOI made clear our goal to develop public policies and catalyze private-sector practices that promote innovation and enhance cybersecurity so that the Internet remains fertile ground for an expanding range of beneficial commercial, civic, and social activity. [8]

Several responses to the NOI suggested that the U.S. continue to treat the Internet with a light touch approach to regulation. [9] Many comments also focused on how to promote voluntary actions through proper incentives, rather than regulation. [10] While a common threat exists across sectors of the economy, a range of approaches is needed to address concerns within sectors. In particular, certain industries are important to innovation and economic growth and may be more responsive to flexible structures for promoting security that is in their own interest. Government should work with these industries to help develop protections that advance innovation and enhance security on the Internet.

---

[8] DEP'T OF COMMERCE, CYBERSECURITY, INNOVATION AND THE INTERNET ECONOMY, 75 Fed. Reg. 44216 (July 28, 2010) (Notice of Inquiry), *available at* http://www.ntia.doc.gov/frnotices/2010/FR_CybersecurityNOI_07282010.pdf. Comments received in response to the NOI and referred to in this Green Paper are available at http://www.nist.gov/itl/cybercomments.cfm.
[9] *See, e.g.*, Online Trust Alliance Comment at 6; Richard Lamb Comment at 12.
[10] *See, e.g.*, ISACA Comment at 6;TechAmerica Comment at 27; Triad Biometrics Comment at 2.

II. Defining the Internet and Information Innovation Sector

In order to focus our attention on this space more clearly, the Task Force determined that it is important to frame and target a new sector that falls outside the classification of covered critical infrastructure.[11] The Task Force is calling this sector the Internet and Information Innovation Sector (I3S). This business sector includes functions and services that fall outside the classification of covered critical infrastructure, create or utilize the Internet and have a large potential for growth, entrepreneurship, and vitalization of the economy. More specifically, the following functions and services are included in the I3S:

- provision of information services and content;
- facilitation of the wide variety of transactional services available through the Internet as an intermediary;
- storage and hosting of publicly accessible content; and
- support of users' access to content or transaction activities, including, but not limited to application, browser, social network, and search providers.

If there is a common theme throughout the record in this inquiry, it is that both the cyber threat environment and the Internet economy remain highly dynamic. Consequently, any policies adopted to mitigate threats in the I3S should minimize their potential dampening effect on Internet commerce. In this vein, commenters also asked that the U.S. government continually enhance its leadership role in the global cybersecurity dialogue, that it promote globally harmonized approaches to cybersecurity, and that it discourage policy initiatives that threaten to balkanize the cybersecurity and associated legal landscape.

The intent of this Green Paper is to stimulate further discussion by reporting on the Task Force's preliminary findings and continuing the consultation process that began with the NOI and the accompanying symposium. We are therefore seeking comments on the definition of the I3S and the vision for the policies to protect the sector. As the Task Force continues to discuss these policy areas, it will coordinate its efforts closely with the White House and other federal agencies that offer their own leadership in this area.

---

[11] The term "covered critical infrastructure" is based on the Administration's legislative proposal delivered to Congress on May 12, 2011. See Howard Schmidt, "The Administration Unveils its Cybersecurity Legislative Proposal," White House Blog, May 12, 2011, available at http://www.whitehouse.gov/blog/2011/05/12/administration-unveils-its-cybersecurity-legislative-proposal.

Questions/Areas for Additional Comment:
- How should the Internet and Information Innovation Sector be defined? What kinds of entities should be included or excluded? How can its functions and services be clearly distinguished from critical infrastructure?
- Is Commerce's focus on an Internet and Information Innovation Sector the right one to target the most serious cybersecurity threats to the Nation's economic and social well-being related to non-critical infrastructure?
- What are the most serious cybersecurity threats facing the I3S as currently defined?
- Are there other sectors not considered critical infrastructure where similar approaches might be appropriate?
- Should I3S companies that also offer functions and services to covered critical infrastructure be treated differently than other members of the I3S?

III. Facing the Challenges of Cybersecurity: Developing Policy Recommendations for the Future

A. *Creating a nationally recognized approach to minimize vulnerabilities for the I3S*

1. Developing and Promoting I3S- Specific Voluntary Codes of Conduct

In the I3S, firms often lack a mechanism for establishing common cybersecurity practices, [12] promoting widely accepted standards or undertaking other cooperative action against specific threats in this area. Where coordination has happened, it has mostly been by volunteers and advocates through newly created groups such as the Messaging Anti-Abuse Working Group (MAAWG), the Anti-Phishing Working Group or the Anti-Spyware Coalition. One possible reason why consistent coordination has not always taken place is the absence of cost-effective institutional mechanisms for setting cybersecurity standards and practices within, and especially across, industries.

---

[12] Throughout this paper, we use terms "codes of conduct," "practices," "standards," and "guidelines" in precise and consistent ways that can be understood by both security experts and in their colloquial use. Please see Appendix B for more context into these different terms.

Several of the comments received from the NOI process stressed the use of voluntary efforts as the best means to create principles and guidelines for promoting cybersecurity among what are essentially parts of the I3S.[13]

As one possible path forward, we seek additional comment on whether to facilitate the establishment, at the federal level, a broadly stated, uniform set of cyber management principles for I3S entities to follow. These voluntary codes of conduct, developed through multi-stakeholder processes and implemented by individual companies will help to provide more certainty for a marketplace where consumer protection, securities and related law are already enforced today.[14] Once these codes have been developed to and companies have committed to follow them, relevant law enforcement agencies, such as Federal Trade Commission (FTC) and State Attorneys General, could enforce them, eventually leading to norms of behavior promoting trust in the consumer marketplace.

For example, federal and state unfair and deceptive acts and practices statutes are enforced against companies that do not adequately secure consumer information.[15] The FTC's enforcement authority stems from Section 5 of the FTC Act, which declares unlawful all "unfair or deceptive acts or practices in or affecting commerce."[16] In order for the FTC to assert that a commercial practice is "unfair," the consumer injury that results from the practice must be substantial, without corresponding benefits, and one that consumers cannot reasonably avoid.[17] Similarly, the FTC will bring an action against a company for engaging in a deceptive trade practice if the company makes a representation; that representation is likely to mislead reasonable consumers; and the representation is material.[18] Using its authority, the FTC has brought several enforcement actions against companies for failing to safeguard consumer data

---

[13] *See* MAAWG Comment at 5-6. *See generally* Information Technology Industry Council, *The IT Industry's Cybersecurity Principles for Industry and Government* (2011), *available at* http://www.itic.org/clientuploads/ITI%20-%20Cybersecurity%20Principles%20for%20Industry%20and%20Government%20-%20Final1.31.11.pdf and the Open Web Application Security Project, *OWASP Application Security Principles* (2011), available at http://www.owasp.org/index.php/Category:Principle.

[14] We expect that cybersecurity frameworks that are developed for the critical infrastructure can help inform standards and practices for non-critical infrastructure companies, including functions and services in the I3S.

[15] *See, e.g.,* 15 U.S.C. § 45(a) (2006); CAL. BUS. & PROF. CODE § 17500 *et seq.* (West 2010).

[16] 15 U.S.C. § 45(a).

[17] 15 U.S.C. § 45(n) (stating the FTC requirements for the FTC to utilize its unfairness authority).

[18] FTC Policy Statement on Deception, *appended to* Cliffdale Associates, Inc., 103 F.T.C. 110, 174 (1984), *available at* http://www.ftc.gov/bcp/policystmt/ad-decept.htm (noting the elements the FTC must establish to find a business practice deceptive under §5 of the FTC Act).

through reasonable security measures.[19] Over the past two decades, the FTC has engaged in numerous enforcement actions that have involved security breaches and other cybersecurity issues with a particular focus around personal privacy and data security issues.[20] The FTC's role in challenging both deceptive and unfair acts or practices in the data security area is vital so that companies' voluntary efforts to implement specific cybersecurity best practices are backed by a legal obligation to implement reasonable and appropriate security. Public companies must also comply with the Information Integrity provisions of Sarbanes-Oxley that require management to certify internal controls are in place to address a wide range of issues including data security.[21]

Focusing attention on particular performance measures, as well as widely accepted standards and practices through codes of conduct, could help to encourage wider adoption of good practices and to avoid mandating security requirements on the I3S. Coordinated effort in this area would move past collective action problems to help the sector moving forward, yet still offer accountability. Voluntary codes of conduct can serve this purpose by helping organizations understand what measures should be taken to adequately protect themselves and their customers from the risk of cyber-attack. In addition, these codes of conduct may also prove useful to the FTC in bringing enforcement actions against cybersecurity activities involving deception.

A key role for government is to assist industry in developing these voluntary codes of conduct. These codes of conduct should aim to unify various technical standards that currently exist and identify a broad set of responsibilities that industry members can use as a baseline for their own cybersecurity efforts. These codes of conduct should also be developed transparently, through a process that is open to all stakeholders including industry members, government, and consumer groups.

Historically, NIST has focused on facilitating the development of voluntary, consensus-based standards. Working with the private sector

---

[19] *See, e.g.*, Complaint at 1-3, *In the Matter of BJ's Wholesale Club, Inc.*, (No. C-4148), 2005 WL 2395788 (F.T.C.), *available at* http://www.ftc.gov/os/caselist/0423160/092305comp0423160.pdf (alleging that BJ's engaged in an unfair practice by failing to take reasonable data security measures); Complaint at 2-5, *In the Matter of Twitter, Inc.*, (No. C-4316), 2011 WL 914034 (F.T.C.), *available at* http://www.ftc.gov/os/caselist/0923093/110311twittercmpt.pdf (attacking Twitter's data security practices as deceptive).

[20] *See* Footnote [citation to BJ's Wholesale and Twitter, currently FN 8 in this document] and accompanying text.

[21] 15 U.S.C. § 7262

and federal agencies. NIST has enabled effective coordination, while allowing for ongoing marketplace developments and technological evolution and innovation. The Department of Commerce proposes to follow this model.

For example, NIST assists in similar efforts through the development of guidelines and convening private-sector participants to address Smart Grid and Health IT cybersecurity issues on an expedited basis. One option is for the Department of Commerce to take similar approaches in the development of voluntary codes of conduct for relevant parts of the I3S where NIST would, consistent with antitrust and other laws, convene groups for certain subsectors.

Policy Recommendation A1:

The Department of Commerce should convene and facilitate members of the I3S to develop voluntary codes of conduct. Where subsectors (such as those with a large number of small businesses) lack the resources to establish their own codes of conduct, NIST may develop guidelines to help aid in bridging that gap. Additionally, the U.S. government should work internationally to advance codes of conduct in ways that are consistent with and/or influence and improve global norms and practices.

Questions/Areas for Additional Comment:

- Are there existing codes of conduct that the I3S can utilize that adequately address these issues?
- Are there existing overarching security principles on which to base codes of conduct?
- What is the best way to solicit and incorporate the views of small and medium businesses into the process to develop codes?
- What is the best way to solicit and incorporate the views of consumers and civil society?
- How should the U.S. government work internationally to advance codes of conduct in ways that are consistent with and/or influence and improve global norms and practices?

2. Promoting Existing Keystone Standards and Practices

The building blocks for codes of conduct are the many existing standards and practices promoted and utilized by security experts. In response to our NOI, many respondents recommended leaving to the private sector the development of Internet security tools that could make up the basis for these voluntary codes of conduct primarily.

It is clear that the government should not be in the business of picking technology winners and losers; however, where consensus emerges that a particular standard or practice will markedly improve the Nation's collective security, the government should consider more proactively promoting industry-led efforts and widely accepted standards and practices and calling on entities to implement them. The Department of Commerce plans, consistent with anti-trust laws, to better promote these efforts as a starting point to building better general industry practices.

There are numerous approaches available today that are widely recognized as best practices, which either are or could be utilized broadly by industry as baselines for security implementations. For example, VeriSign cited in their NOI submission the "Twenty Critical Controls for Effective Cyber Defense Consensus Audit Guidelines,"[22] developed in August 2009, as an example of security controls spanning a wide range of threats.[23]

While many of these standards and practices target particular sectors or entities, many are widely applicable beyond their intended targets and often provide far-reaching guidelines or baselines for cyber-security best practices.

Broad guidelines or frameworks, existing and under development, that incorporate multiple practices and standards include, but are not limited to the following:

- Payment Card Industry Data Security Standard (PCI DSS) – self-regulatory set of standards and practices developed to help organizations proactively protect financial and other sensitive customer account data.
- NIST Special Publication 800-53 – guidelines for U.S. government agencies, but in wide voluntary use by the private sector, which apply to all components of information systems that process, store, or transmit federal information.
- Identity Management and a National Strategy for Trusted Identities in Cyberspace (NSTIC) – a strategy to establish identity solutions, practices and privacy-enhancing technologies that will improve the security and convenience of sensitive online transactions by

---

[22] VeriSign Comment at 5.
[23] The "Twenty Controls" were developed by the SANS Institute and are available at http://www.sans.org/critical-security-controls/.

enabling improved processes for authenticating individuals, organizations, and underlying infrastructure.

There are also targeted standards aimed at protecting specific areas, such as:

- Internet Protocol Security (via IPSEC) – standards to help ensure private, secure communications (at the packet level) over Internet Protocol (IP) networks.
- Domain Name System Security (via DNSSEC) – protocol extension to better protect the Internet from certain DNS related attacks such as cache poisoning.
- Internet Routing Security – standards to better secure Internet routing by addressing vulnerabilities in the Border Gateway Protocol (BGP).
- Web Security (via SSL and https) – protocols and certificates to better secure Web-based applications and transactions.
- Email Security (via SPF and DKIM) – protocols that authenticate emails (sender and/or content authentication) assisting in the battle against spam and phishers.

The guidelines, standards, and practices listed above are detailed in Appendix B.

The codes of conduct, discussed in section A1, will ultimately need to be based on a set of overarching principles and performance measures as well as detailed standards and practices. It is important to note that while implementation of these guidelines or standards may be necessary to protect security in certain instances, they are almost never sufficient when implemented in isolation. Moreover, particular standards may harden information systems from particular avenues of attack, but may leave other avenues open. Compliance with particular standards or guidelines does not demonstrate that a company's security practices are adequate across the board. While voluntary adoption of best practices would not supplant existing regulatory enforcement regimes, greater adoption of best practices would likely significantly improve security beyond the baseline required by existing law.   While all of the standards and practices outlined in Appendix B are in use today, many are not as widely used as they could be to maximize security across the Internet, thereby offering the best place to start building efforts to create the frameworks that can develop into codes of conduct.

Any code of conduct must be robust and substantive, so that by adopting it, a company is able to materially improve its security practices.   The process for devising codes must also be flexible and nimble enough to ensure that the codes remain effective in an ever-changing security environment.

Policy Recommendation A2:

The Department of Commerce should work with other government, private sector, and non-government organizations to proactively promote keystone standards and practices.

Questions/Areas for Additional Comment:

- Are the standards, practices, and guidelines indicated in this section and detailed in Appendix B appropriate to consider as keystone efforts? Are there others not listed here that should be included?
- Is there a level of consensus today around all or any of these guidelines, practices and standards as having the ability to improve security? If not, is it possible to achieve consensus? If so, how?
- What process should the Department of Commerce use to work with industry and other stakeholders to identify best practices, guidelines, and standards in the future?
- Should efforts be taken to better promote and/or support the adoption of these standards, practices, and guidelines?
- In what way should these standards, practices, and guidelines be promoted and through what mechanisms?
- What incentives are there to ensure that standards are robust? What incentives are there to ensure that best practices and standards, once adopted, are updated in the light of changing threats and new business models?
- Should the government play an active role in promoting these standards, practices, and guidelines? If so, in which areas should the government play more of a leading role? What should this role be?

3. Promoting Automation of Security

Several commenters to the NOI discussed how they use automated methods to detect potentially dangerous web behavior in order to prevent users from exposing themselves to risk suggesting that others could be doing the same. These entities said that they also were providing incentives to the owners of bad websites to reform.[24]

By some accounts, approximately 80 percent of successful online attacks are attributable to known vulnerabilities that can be addressed with implementation of widely agreed upon industry standards, proper configurations and patches. As more computing services are based in the cloud and move further away from centralized enterprises, automating security will likely become even more important than it is today. Enterprise and service delivery will need to address vulnerabilities easily and quickly in order to assure customers of security. In particular, the automated sharing of threats and related signature information among government agencies, among the private sector, and between public and private entities is becoming more commonplace.[25]

With leadership from NIST, the National Security Agency (NSA), DHS and the U.S. CIO Council,[26] the U.S. government leads efforts to automate configuration and vulnerability management. The private sector has also begun to adopt automation protocols such as Security Content Automation Protocol (SCAP) and Continuous Monitoring. These efforts offer enterprises of all sizes the ability to better update security compliance at potentially lower costs and pave the way for future automated protocols.

The security automation initiative is a public/private collaboration that spans multiple government agencies, more than 30 security tool vendors, and a host of end user organizations. The goal of the project is to enable the efficient and accurate collection, correlation, and sharing of security relevant information including software vulnerabilities, system configurations and network events across disparate systems in the enterprise.

Security automation work currently supports reference data such as the National Vulnerability Database (NVD), which provides software vulnerability information to users worldwide, and system configurations such as the U.S. government Configuration Baseline (USGCB) through the

---

[24] *See, e.g.*, Google Comment at 2; Stop Badware Comment at 4.

[25] DHS addressed this issue in detail in its recent White Paper, DEP'T OF HOMELAND SECURITY, ENABLING DISTRIBUTED SECURITY IN CYBERSPACE: BUILDING A HEALTHY AND RESILIENT CYBER ECOSYSTEM WITH AUTOMATED COLLECTIVE ACTION (2011), *available at* http://www.dhs.gov/xlibrary/assets/nppd-cyber-ecosystem-white-paper-03-23-2011.pdf.

[26] *See About CIO*, CIO.GOV, http://www.cio.gov ("CIO.gov is the website of the U.S. CIO and the federal CIO Councils, serving as a central resource for information on federal IT. By showcasing examples of innovation, identifying best practices, and providing a forum for federal IT leaders, CIO.gov keeps the public informed about how our Government is working to close the technology gap between the private and public sectors.").

Technology Infrastructure Sub-committee of the CIO Council. Standardization of security information has created opportunities for innovation in the private sector and research into new information domains like network events and asset management is expected to foster additional innovation in those markets. Through procurement strategies, the U.S. government can continue to provide tools for leveraging security automation technologies, leveraging existing vendor investment while encouraging additional investment in support of new specifications and standards.

Policy Recommendation A3:

The U.S. government should promote and accelerate both public and private sector efforts to research, develop and implement automated security and compliance.

Questions/Areas for Additional Comment:

- How can automated security be improved?
- What areas of research in automation should be prioritized?
- How can the Department of Commerce, working with its partners, better promote automated sharing of threat and related signature information with the I3S?
- Are there other examples of automated security that should be promoted?

4. Improving and modernizing security assurance

Security assurance is an area of cybersecurity that focuses on providing an adequate level of trust that information technology products purchased contain security controls and that those controls function as advertised. There are several security assurance standards, but many commenters to the NOI focused on the International Common Criteria for Information Technology Security Evaluation (commonly known as Common Criteria ISO/IEC 15408). The Common Criteria are a set of security standards adopted by countries where a technology is given a "protection profile" created by a user community and a third party evaluation is done for a company that develops that technology.[27] Most

---

[27] *See, e.g.*, atsec Comment at 5-6; BSA Comment at 8-9; Cisco Comment at 12-13; IBM Comment at 3-5; (ISC)² Comment at 9-10; Smart Card Alliance at 11-13.

respondents agreed the Common Criteria is a productive initiative that should be emulated and further enhanced. Cisco and IBM highlight efficiency and cost benefits from broad standardization of requirements.[28] The U.S. Chamber of Commerce went even further, maintaining that product assurance is vital to national and economic security.[29] Various groups envisioned the specific direction of this standard differently. (ISC)[2] supported Common Criteria product certification, but believes "the process is often too heavy handed and needs to be more agile so that the process is able to meet different levels of need or risk."[30]

Microsoft expressed concern that the standards have not kept pace with the cybersecurity landscape and must evolve more quickly,[31] while the Business Software Alliance (BSA) and TechAmerica advocated for regulations that are transparent and do not favor any particular technologies.[32] Enthusiasm for the Common Criteria is tempered by several related challenges, with PayPal warning that rigid certification standards lead to delayed deployment of essential security patches,[33] and Richard Lamb[34] arguing that even light regulation arising from such standards "would result in stifling innovation and slowing development."[35]

There was a common thread of concern regarding the ability of American companies to sell their products abroad based on the impact of product assurance standards. IBM, for example, suggested that many new problems are arising from foreign countries that "impose nationalistic certificates and requirements" or require government access to intellectual property.[36] These companies saw Common Criteria as a better solution to domestic solutions or demand of access to source code under conditions that do not preserve the integrity of trade secrets that are becoming more common in non-signatory nations. Atsec and the Smart Card Alliance both noted that non-signatory nations may require developers to disclose their intellectual property.[37] International trade was also a concern to the Information Technology Industry Council (ITI), which hopes the federal government will work to expand the Common

---

[28] Cisco Comment at 13; IBM at 5.
[29] U.S. Chamber of Commerce Comment at 4.
[30] *See, e.g.,* (ISC)[2] Comment at 10.
[31] Microsoft Comment at 18.
[32] BSA Comment at 9; TechAmerica Comment at 24.
[33] PayPal Comment at 4.
[34] Richard Lamb is the former Director Global IT Policy at the US Department of State and current DNSSEC Program Manager at ICANN.
[35] Richard Lamb Comment at 12.
[36] IBM Comment at 5.
[37] atsec Comment at 17; Smart Card Alliance Comment at 12.

Criteria Community to preserve the global market. ITI places particular emphasis on the importance of standards that recognize the global nature of the supply chain and prevent its hindrance.[38] The Common Criteria would, in Microsoft's view, lead "users and suppliers [to] benefit if product assurance criteria and evaluation regimes are harmonized globally."[39]

Finally, a few respondents commented more specifically on what would constitute best practices for any product assurance framework with flexibility based on risk and value of the systems being protected. Synaptic made the case that security certification should include independent penetration testing – in other words, independent experts should simulate attempts to gain illicit access to systems in addition to more conventional product assurance activities.[40] The BSA and TechAmerica also advocated a practical approach, noting that good assurance mechanisms "can usefully address questions of what threats need to be considered and the degree of confidence that the product actually addresses these threats"[41] and "may also include verifying that a product not only does what it was designed to do, but also does not do what it was *not* designed to do."[42] Noting that it has developed a useful framework to serve this purpose, the Internet Security Alliance argued that supply chain audits are essential to assuring the security of final products.[43] Other respondents echoed this recommendation, calling for study of the origin of malware within supply chains, as well as ways in which malware is developed and spread.[44] Atsec believed that a breakthrough in combating cybercrime will only occur when IT systems are "analyzed for their security impact starting at the early stages of the design and traced down to the implementation."[45]

The Department of Commerce believes that third party conformance assessment is a useful means to build security compliance, but its current application for security assurance needs to be adapted to remain relevant. In particular, lessons must be learned from the Common Criteria. Adding another wrinkle, to secure I3S functions and services, a more dynamic and cost effective assurance structure may be more necessary than for technologies designed for critical infrastructure, albeit the U.S. Government, like the private sector, is heavily reliant on commercial products and have similar requirements. Efforts to improve

---

[38] ITI Comment at 5.
[39] Microsoft Comment at 18.
[40] Synaptic Comment at 13.
[41] BSA Comment at 8.
[42] TechAmerica Comment at 23.
[43] Internet Security Alliance Comment at 27.
[44] *See, e.g.*, Cyveillance Comment at 2; VeriSign Comment at 3.
[45] atsec Comment at 4.

existing assurance models in the private sector and among government agencies are important for the future of security efforts in both sectors.

Policy Recommendation A4:

The Department of Commerce, in concert with other agencies and the private sector, should work to improve and augment conformance-based assurance models for their IT systems.

Questions/Areas for Additional Comment:

- What conformance-based assurance programs, in government or the private sector need to be harmonized?
- In a fast changing/evolving security threat environment, how can security efforts be determined to be relevant and effective? What are the best means to review procedural improvements to security assurance and compliance for capability to pace with technological changes that impact the I3S and other sectors?

B. *Building incentives for I3S to combat cybersecurity threats*

1. Develop the right mix of incentives to promote adoption of cybersecurity best practices.

Even the most effective means for cybersecurity are useless if entities do not adopt them. It is necessary to develop measures rapidly to better protect the Internet, but to date many solutions have failed to provide sufficient incentives for firms to ingrain cybersecurity best practices into their operations.

The Information Systems Audit and Control Association (ISACA) noted that "the challenge in cybersecurity is not that best practices need to be developed," but instead lies in "communicating those best practices, demonstrating the value of implementing them, and encouraging individuals and organizations to adopt them."[46] While others echoed these sentiments in response to the NOI, there was little agreement

---

[46] ISACA Comment at 6.

among respondents on how to provide proper incentives for I3S to adopt cybersecurity best practices.

Commenters identified several methods to incentivize companies to adopt cybersecurity best practices. For example, TechAmerica and Triad Biometrics agreed that tax incentives, government procurement, and streamlined regulatory requirements would be most effective incentives to encourage adoption of best practices.[47] TechAmerica specifically advised that "ways to devise a refundable tax credit for cybersecurity investments should be explored."[48] The Internet Security Alliance also included liability protection, SBA loans, stimulus grants, and insurance as other alternatives to support I3S adoption of best practices.[49]

With respect to safe-harbors, some companies supported them as a means of encouraging I3S to utilize a critical minimum set of security standards and practices, but expressed concern that "compliance with [potential safe-harbor requirements] could result in wasted or misdirected investment in unnecessary and/or outdated security measures as well as [provide] a false sense of security."[50] By contrast, one commenter suggested that there is little merit in introducing legal safe-harbors by regulation.[51] Instead, "the legal system should develop such treatments organically as cases make their way through the courts."[52] Because, as Verisign noted, ill-fashioned legal safe-harbors may create a false sense of security,[53] legal safe-harbors could actually reduce incentives for I3S to adopt all reasonable cybersecurity measures because they might implement an insufficient set of measures that, although potentially limiting their liability, would not reduce other harms that could accrue as a result of cyber attacks. Also, as noted above, governmental enforcement of legal requirements that companies implement reasonable and appropriate security is a key backstop for implementation of good security practices. Therefore, questions remain about whether legal safe-harbors are an effective way to promote I3S adoption of best practices, and how safe-harbors could be fashioned to avoid creating reverse incentives that would cause I3S to implement only the bare minimum in preventative cybersecurity measures.

Several respondents to the NOI suggested that another way to promote market-wide adoption of better standards and practices could be to

---

[47] *See, e.g.,* TechAmerica Comment at 27; Triad Biometrics Comment at 2.
[48] TechAmerica Comment at 27.
[49] Internet Security Alliance at 36.
[50] VeriSign Comment at 2, 7.
[51] Richard Lamb Comment at 15.
[52] *Id.*
[53] Verisign Comment at 7.

couple their use with cyberinsurance.[54] Indeed, if entities can clearly identify their risk of liability – through, for example, expectations of personal loss or anticipated legal liability, cyberinsurance may be an effective, market-driven way of increasing cybersecurity because it can:

- reduce the incidence of cyber attacks by promoting widespread adoption of preventative measures throughout the market;
- encourage the adoption of best practices because "[c]yberinsurers can actually promote self-protection by basing cyberinsurance premiums on the insured's level of self-protection."[55]; and
- limit the level of losses I3S may face following a cyber attack.

For example, Jean Bolot and Marc Lelarge concluded that cyberinsurance premiums, like premiums in other insurance markets, "should be negatively related to the amount invested by the user in security (self-protection)."[56] This result "parallels the real life situation where homeowners who invest in a burglar alarm and new locks expect their [homeowners insurance] premium to decrease as a result of their investment."[57]

In 2009, market researchers estimated that the national market for cyberinsurance ranged from $450 to $500 million.[58] This represented an increase of $100 million from four years earlier, when the market for cyberinsurance was estimated at between $350 and $400 million.[59] Research suggests that the cyberinsurance market has not grown more

---

[54] *See, e.g.,* CyberRisk Partners Comment at 1; Internet Security Alliance Comment at 36. CyberRisk Partners expressed the belief that "public policy should play as little role as possible in the development of a cyber-risk measurement framework." CyberRisk Partners Comment at 1. While the Department of Commerce agrees that government should play a limited role in the further development of the cyberinsurance market, we do believe that government can provide meaningful assistance to the industry in overcoming coordination problems that likely exist in the market. For example, government can help aggregate information about what types of data, actuarials, and other research is necessary to grow the market and ensure that cyberinsurance promotes the widespread adoption of security best practices, and adequately addresses I3S needs.

[55] Kesan et al., *Three Economic Arguments for Cyberinsurance, in* SECURING PRIVACY IN THE INTERNET AGE 345, 350 (2008).

[56] Jean Bolot and Marc Lelarge, *Cyber Insurance as an Incentive for Internet Security*, in MANAGING INFORMATION RISK AND THE ECONOMICS OF SECURITY 269, 271 (2009).

[57] *Id.*

[58] Frank Innerhofer & Ruth Breu, *Potential Rating Indicators for Cyberinsurance: An Exploratory Qualitative Study, in* ECONOMICS OF INFORMATION SECURITY & PRIVACY 249, 250 (Tyler Moore et al. eds., 2010). This figure represents an estimate of the total amount of cyberinsurance premiums paid by companies in the U.S. during the 2009 calendar year, based on a market research survey.

[59] George Mason University School of Law, Critical Infrastructure Protection Program, *The CIP Report,* at 2 (2007), *available at* http://cip.gmu.edu/archive/cip_report_6.3.pdf.

rapidly because cyber insurers "still struggle to determine appropriate premium rates for covering cyber risks."[60] This difficulty arises from a general lack of data – both actuarial data regarding the losses that result from cyber attacks and statistical data regarding the frequency of cybersecurity incidents.[61] For cyber-insurance to be an effective tool in encouraging the adoption of best practices, cyber insurers should conduct further research on authoritative risk indicators; compile data on security breaches and the implementation of preventative measures; and develop actuarials that accurately assess the risk of cyber threats and the cost of harms that result from online attacks.

Scholars have suggested that "[i]n pricing [any] premium, it is essential [for insurers] to identify the likelihood of a potential disaster as well as its impact."[62] Although there is relatively limited research on the appropriate metrics to determine cyber-insurance premiums, one recent, qualitative study that polled European risk experts[63] identified and ranked a list of ninety-four risk indicators, including first-party loss indicators, third-party loss indicators, and indicators regarding the quality of IT Risk Management.[64] This study found two of the most highly ranked indicators of first-party loss to be the extent of a company's critical dependency of business processes on IT, and the degree to which companies' process highly confidential and sensitive data.[65] Similarly, the quality of patch-management for information systems was a strong indicator of third-party loss exposure.[66] Finally, the existence of a dedicated "risk officer" within an organization was the strongest indicator of quality cyber risk management.[67] Other researchers have found that the harm resulting from a cyber attack often correlates strongly with the type of computer affected by a security incident.[68]

Such research studies can provide valuable insights and data to help cyber insurers identify the risk factors most closely associated with a potential cybersecurity incident. Further research by the academic community and insurance industry can aid in our understanding of best

---

[60] Innerhofer & Breu, *supra* note 72, at 250.

[61] *Id.* at 250.

[62] Hemantha S. B. Herath & Tejaswini Herath, *Cyber-Insurance: Copula Pricing Framework and Implications for Risk Management*, WORKSHOP ECON. & INFO. SEC. 1, 4 (2007), *available at* http://weis2007.econinfosec.org/papers/24.pdf.

[63] For this study, researchers conducted interviews with thirty-six risk management experts in the DACH region (i.e., experts in Germany, Switzerland, and Austria).

[64] Innerhofer & Breu, *supra* note 58 at 264-66.

[65] *Id.* at 264.

[66] *Id.* at 265.

[67] *Id.* at 266.

[68] Herath & Heratch, *supra* note 62, at 4.

practices that can deter future cyber attacks or reduce their impact. Additional research studies should examine whether the risk indicators identified in the foregoing study are equally indicative of cybersecurity risks for American companies, and should identify indicators that are more applicable to the cybersecurity climate in the American market. Further research should study other risk indicators identified in the study conducted by Professors Innerhofer and Breu.[69] For example, does the mere presence of a dedicated risk officer decrease the risk of cyber attack? Or, is the level of risk correlated more strongly with the officer's attentiveness in implementing best practices and other preventative measures?

Once industry stakeholders develop appropriate metrics for measuring the risk of cybersecurity attacks and the harm that results from security incidents, companies should be encouraged to compile and share this data. Increased information sharing will enable cyber insurers to agree on authoritative ways to assess risk. To aid in this effort, the Internet Security Alliance has proposed that SBA loans and stimulus funding be used to encourage I3S to report cyber attacks.[70] Downstream, increases in information sharing and reporting will help cyber insurers understand how to set insurance premiums at market-appropriate levels, and determine standards and practices that should be coupled with cyberinsurance offerings.

Additionally, once cyberinsurers understand how to quantify the risk of cyber attacks and the harm caused by incidents, the market can determine the appropriate price for premiums. Premiums should be set at a level that will not only encourage cyber insurers to offer full liability coverage, but at a level that will also encourage I3S to implement cybersecurity best practices, either in addition, or as a prerequisite to obtaining cyberinsurance coverage. Through this avenue, I3S will begin to recognize the externalities that result from cyber attacks and acknowledge, financially, how these indirect costs impact their organization.

Despite the concerns raised above, carefully tailored incentives such as cyber-insurance, tax incentives, and related legislation could have a potential to promote increased adoption of cybersecurity best practices that could lead to a long-term, reduction in the overall incidence and harm caused by cyber attacks, but clearly more research is needed. Through such measures, I3S could be able to rely more on the marketplace to develop and implement preventative cybersecurity

---

[69] *See generally* Innerhofer & Breu, supra note 58.
[70] Internet Security Alliance Comment at 29.

measures, and can better manage their potential exposure to financial liability.

In general, many of the incentive suggestions that the Department of Commerce received through the NOI were too high level to be actionable. For example, tax incentives are clearly popular, but no commenter offered anticipated costs or offered suggestions on how costs could be offset. Similarly, cyberinsurance offers the possibility of creating better incentives, but no commenter had detailed solutions to address problems such as adequately evaluating risk. Therefore, the best conclusion to draw from the NOI responses is that more information is needed to move proposals such as these forward.

Policy Recommendation B1:

The Department of Commerce and industry should continue to explore and identify incentives to encourage I3S to adopt voluntary cybersecurity best practices.

Questions/Areas for Additional Comment:
- What are the right incentives to gain adoption of best practices? What are the right incentives to ensure that the voluntary codes of conduct that develop from best practices are sufficiently robust? What are the right incentives to ensure that codes of conduct, once introduced, are updated promptly to address evolving threats and other changes in the security environment?
- How can the Department of Commerce or other government agencies encourage I3S subsectors to build appropriate best practices?
- How can liability structures and insurance be used as incentives to protect the I3S?
- What other market tools are available to encourage cybersecurity best practices?
- Should federal procurement play any role in creating incentives for the I3S? If so, how? If not, why not?

2. Using security disclosure as an incentive

In its Green Paper on commercial data privacy, the Task Force endorsed the adoption of transparency and disclosure of information practices as an important measure. The Task Force also endorsed a national cyber breach notification law such as those currently pending before Congress and the concept has been supported by the Administration.[71] While that Green Paper focused on the privacy benefit of disclosure of breaches, it is difficult to overlook the benefit to security as well. The disclosures, serving as a light handed negative incentive, seem to encourage firms to better secure the personal information that they hold about individuals and take steps to prevent the breaches that cause them.

State-level security breach notification laws have been successful in directing private-sector resources to protecting personal data and reducing the number of breaches, but the differences among these state laws present undue costs to American businesses.[72] A legislated and comprehensive national approach to commercial data breach will provide clarity to individuals regarding the protection of their information throughout the United States, streamline industry compliance, and allow businesses to develop a strong, nationwide data management strategy.

More generally, the BSA expressed support in their comments for "a single national framework for notification of breaches where there is a significant risk of sensitive personally identifiable information being used to harm."[73] The Chamber of Commerce echoed this readiness-focused sentiment, and supported "greater regulation to supply cybersecurity as a public good."[74]

MAAWG stressed that the best cybersecurity incentive is for government to "increase transparency and accuracy with respect to the Internet names and numbers it oversees," which would allow the community to "make informed decisions about their online neighbors."[75]

In other areas, government bodies have been able to create incentives for similar companies to protect individuals simply by providing greater disclosure of practices. For example, Europe and the United States have environmental laws requiring companies to disclose potentially toxic particulate releases. The EU recently passed a law requiring customers to be notified upon a breach of personal data by ISPs that is similar in some ways to successful state laws in the United States. Also, in 1998, the FTC

---

[71] DEP'T OF COMMERCE, COMMERCIAL DATA PRIVACY AND INNOVATION IN THE INTERNET ECONOMY: A DYNAMIC POLICY FRAMEWORK (2010) [hereinafter PRIVACY GREEN PAPER], *available at* http://www.ntia.doc.gov/reports/2010/IPTF_Privacy_GreenPaper_12162010.pdf.at 37.
[72] *See, for example,* Ponemon Institute and Symantec, 2010 ANNUAL STUDY: U.S. COST OF A DATA BREACH – COMPLIANCE PRESSURES, CYBER ATTACKS TARGETING SENSITIVE DATA DRIVE LEADING IT ORGANIZATIONS TO RESPOND QUICKLY AND PAY MORE (2011) *available at* http://www.symantec.com/content/en/us/about/media/pdfs/symantec_ponemon_data _breach_costs_report.pdf.
[73] BSA Comment at 11.
[74] U.S. Chamber of Commerce Comment at 5.
[75] MAAWG Comment at 9.

requested information on Web privacy policies, which has been credited for increasing the percentage of websites with privacy policies from 17 percent to 67 percent in one year and to over 90 percent in every subsequent survey.

The Administration believes that disclosure of cybersecurity plans and evaluations would be an effective tool to promote better security in critical infrastructure. The disclosure of cybersecurity plans and evaluations will allow markets and other firms, the government, and the public at large to hold owners of critical infrastructure accountable for running cybersecurity risks or face liability.[76] We seek additional comment on how such a similar policy tool might be used more expansively within the I3S.

The Department of Commerce could also create surveys to support requirements for standards and practices such as those outlined in Appendix B. The goal of the surveys would be to support evaluation of applicability for some of the widely agreed upon security standards and practices for non-critical infrastructure companies such as those discussed earlier in this paper. The results of the study would be released in aggregate and, eventually, companies not in compliance could be identified as a way to provide an incentive for companies to improve their practices.

Policy Recommendation B2a:

Congress should enact into law a commercial data security breach framework for electronic records that includes notification provisions, encourages companies to implement strict data security protocols, and allows states to build upon the framework in defined ways. The legislation should track the effective protections that have emerged from state security breach notification laws and policies.

Policy Recommendation B2b:

The Department of Commerce should urge the I3S to voluntarily disclose their cybersecurity plans where such disclosure can be used as a means

---

[76] Howard Schmidt, "The Administration Unveils its Cybersecurity Legislative Proposal," White House Blog, May 12, 2011, available at http://www.whitehouse.gov/blog/2011/05/12/administration-unveils-its-cybersecurity-legislative-proposal.

to increase accountability, and where disclosure of those plans are not already required.

Questions/Areas for Additional Comment:

- How important is the role of disclosure of security practices in protecting the I3S? Will it have a significant financial or operational impact?
- Should an entity's customers, patients, clients, etc. receive information regarding the entity's compliance with certain standards and codes of conduct?
- Would it be more appropriate for some types of companies within the I3S be required to create security plans and disclose them to a government agency or to the public? If so, should such disclosure be limited to where I3S services or functions impact certain areas of the covered critical infrastructure?

3. Facilitating Information Sharing and Other Public/Private Partnerships in the I3S to Improve Cybersecurity

Considering the public-private nature of the Internet and its use in the United States, it is natural to consider public-private partnerships as a means for encouraging adoption of security best practices and providing incentives for incident information sharing. Sharing threat and other cybersecurity information between the I3S and agencies with cybersecurity authorities and among I3S entities, implemented consistent with the antitrust laws and privacy concerns, could significantly aid in limiting vulnerabilities, preventing attacks, stopping cybercrime, and catching perpetrators.

Key to raising awareness and adoption of best practices is better understanding what the threats are. As pointed out by (ISC)² in their comments, "[w]e have long been challenged by the inability to share useful and actionable threat information between industry and government, but [that] we need to find a way to do it."[77] According to VeriSign, impediments to cooperation and information sharing include "no clear division of responsibility for incidents, differences in the

---

[77] (ISC)² Comment at 5.

security cultures of the relevant parties, lack of trust relationships between partners, and no common information sharing model."[78]

A number of NOI respondents called attention to the fact that there currently exist a number of entities and programs (both public and private) with the responsibilities of collecting, disseminating, and/or acting upon incident information.[79] Several respondents suggested that the public and private sectors would be better served by devoting their focus and limited resources to fewer, more coordinated programs. According to AT&T, it should be the public policy of the United States to leverage and consolidate existing public and private sector efforts, encourage the use of best practices, and to develop a way for the public and private sectors to share relevant cyber threat information in real-time. Underlying this and other similar comments was the critical need not to duplicate existing efforts.[80]

Some respondents, including the Center for Democracy and Technology (CDT), cautioned that any improvements to existing information sharing mechanisms need to proceed incrementally. CDT questioned the effectiveness of existing mechanisms and recommended the preliminary step of undertaking a thorough analysis to determine what information should be shared, as well as to understand why existing public-private partnerships such as the Information Sharing and Analysis Centers (ISACs) are not working the way they should.[81]

In terms of potential public-private partnership models to be explored moving forward, VeriSign indicated the desirability to develop an overall framework of information sharing, with a single authority for gathering information on cyber crime incidents for e-commerce. One option they put forward is the creation of "an e-commerce ISAC, as none of the other 17 ISACs specifically serve the e-commerce community."[82] It was the view of Microsoft that any effective public-private partnership framework focused on "[i]mproving collaboration and operational information sharing requires dedicated efforts to enhance: [e]xchange of technical data . . . with rules and mechanisms that permit both [the public and private] sides to protect their sensitive data"; "[j]oint analysis of risks . . . and development of mitigation strategies"; and "[f]urther innovation in threat reduction efforts to ensure the security of the broader ecosystem."[83]

---

[78] Verisign Comment at 2.
[79] See, e.g., (ISC)² Comment at 3; Microsoft at 10.
[80] AT&T Comment at 19.
[81] *See, e.g.*, CDT Comment at 4-5.
[82] Verisign Comment at 2-3.
[83] Microsoft Comment at 8.

The issue of relevance, value, and resources to participate in information sharing is important to address, particularly the context of the I3S sector. As noted by TechAmerica, a great majority of small and medium-sized businesses across the country are not familiar with public-private mechanisms available. Even if they are aware, their ability to participate may be low due to cost or to finding prioritized benefit and relevance. TechAmerica recommended finding "ways to adjust the partnership structure to accommodate the specific needs of small and medium sized businesses."[84]

Commenters said that a central tenet of a public-private information sharing mechanism is that it be voluntary and self-regulatory. Network Solutions noted that strong self-regulatory regimes have the advantages of being flexible and adaptable to new developments and emerging threats.[85] They suggested that through self-regulation, industry is able to dialogue with governmental agencies to address concerns proactively and productively. A role for government, according to the Online Trust Alliance, is to "endorse and raise awareness of existing information sharing architectures and encourage companies to voluntarily participate, rather than regulatory compliance and reporting."[86]

Policy Recommendation B3:

The Department of Commerce should work with other agencies, organizations, and other relevant entities of the I3S to build and/or improve upon existing public-private partnerships that can help promote information sharing.

Questions/Areas for Additional Comment:

- What role can the Department of Commerce play in promoting public-private partnerships?
- How can public-private partnerships be used to foster better incentives within the I3S?
- How can existing public-private partnerships be improved?
- What are the barriers to information sharing between the I3S and government agencies with cybersecurity authorities and among I3S entities? How can they be overcome?

---

[84] TechAmerica Comment at 8.
[85] Network Solutions Comment at 2.
[86] Online Trust Alliance Comment at 3.

- Do current liability structures create a disincentive to participate in information sharing or other best practice efforts?

C. *Education and Research*

Preserving innovation as well as private sector and consumer confidence in the security of the Internet economy is important for promoting economic prosperity and social well-being. Public policies and private-sector practices that promote education and innovation for the purpose of enhancing cybersecurity will help ensure that the Internet remains fertile ground for an expanding range of beneficial commercial and social activity. The Department of Commerce recognizes the valuable roles, responsibilities, and capabilities of the private sector in building research to mitigate cyber risks associated with the Internet. More broadly, over the past two decades, the nation has benefited greatly from industry-led, Internet-driven innovation and growth, with those benefits reflected throughout the entire economy.

That said, the persistence and growth of cybersecurity threats compels us to re-think both how those challenges are affecting U.S. businesses and citizens, as well as useful steps that can enhance the security of Internet-based commerce. Small, medium, and large businesses, and consumers, will continue to increase their reliance on the Internet increasing the size of the I3S. As that reliance grows, their understanding of cybersecurity must increase as well. The Department of Commerce believes that public policies affecting cybersecurity on the Internet, as well as private sector norms, must be continually updated to remain relevant in a fast changing environment.

1. Develop Better Cost/Benefit Analysis for I3S Security

Through the NOI, the Department of Commerce sought comment on how to quantify the macro-and typical micro-economic impact of cyber-incidents, since it is often said that one cannot manage a problem if one cannot measure it. Synaptic Laboratories, for example, remarked that "without such information it is not possible to make an informed decision about the necessary level of security mechanisms required."[87] According to atsec, measuring the cost-effectiveness of security measures is particularly difficult, if not impossible, without quantitative data.[88] While these issues play directly into the cybersecurity insurance discussion, they are also essential for a more general understanding of

---

[87] Synaptic Comment at 3.
[88] atsec Comment at 4.

where research is necessary and where the greatest need for education efforts lie.

Despite that request, most respondents agreed that the economic impact of inadequate cybersecurity is unknown due to the lack of available data. Closing this knowledge gap, however, will be no simple task. The Department of Commerce received a range of views on how best to approach this problem. One respondent recommended directly polling end-users or owners of data to determine the sustained perceived economic loss.[89] For a practical method of measuring economic impact, another commenter similarly recommended using statistical sampling instead of relying on an expensive "100% approach."[90]

Creating an appropriate measurement methodology will require great care. For instance, one commenter argued that the damage to companies from security breaches is easily quantifiable, but the cost to individuals whose information has been compromised is hard to measure.[91] Some respondents identified specific areas, such as the impact of intellectual property loss, where additional data could be collected and used to better understand the economic consequences.[92] Commenters further suggested gathering data from information and communication service providers on industry best practices and on the presence of Information Security Policies. VeriSign also advocated for measuring the time that elapses between the compromising of a system and detection of the breach, known as "compromise to discovery."[93] Other issues may require robust protections for proprietary information and possible changes in the law. All such information is likely to be considered business-confidential at the firm level. So, overcoming impediments to collecting data may require amendments to existing privacy and data protection laws.[94]

Several respondents recommended the development of a comprehensive information collection framework, featuring "a single authority for gathering information on cyber crime incidents" to be aggregated for economic and other analysis.[95] Microsoft advocated working in parallel with the Department of Justice, the Bureau of Economic Analysis, and the DHS to better track and measure cybercrime activity and its negative economic impact.[96] This echoed a theme throughout the comments that

---

[89] CyberRisk Partners Comment at 3.
[90] atsec Comment at 3.
[91] Triad Biometrics Comment at 1.
[92] (ISC)² Comment at 4.
[93] *See, e.g.,* Verisign Comment at 3.
[94] *Id.* at 2.
[95] *See, e.g., Id.* at 3.
[96] Microsoft Comment at 3.

the federal government ought to work hard to constrain and, wherever possible, reduce the federal points-of-contact on cybersecurity issues, so that coordination is less fragmented and less daunting to the public.

Policy Recommendation C1:

The Department of Commerce should work across government and with the private sector to build a stronger understanding (at both the firm and at the macro-economic level) of the costs of cyber threats and the benefits of greater security to the I3S.

Questions/Areas for Additional Comment:

- What is the best means to promote research on cost/benefit analyses for I3S security?
- Are there any examples of new research on cost/benefit analyses of I3S security? In particular, has any of this research significantly changed the understanding of cybersecurity and cybersecurity related decision-making?
- What information is needed to build better cost/benefit analyses?

2. Creating and Measuring I3S Cybersecurity Education Efforts

Public awareness of cybersecurity issues is at the core of our evolving strategy to enhance online safety. As attacks on consumers and corporations become more commonplace and sophisticated, there must be increased preparedness to respond to and mitigate these attacks that can harm the economy, public safety, and our spirit of innovation. While education of the public may offer limited effectiveness in safeguarding against some threats (such as massive data breaches, carding markets, sophisticated point of sale or ATM scams), other common threats (such as malware, fraudulent websites, viruses, phishing or spear phishing emails, and the exploitation of vulnerabilities in servers and network infrastructure) often do take advantage of the lack of education of individuals. While research and development are important to preventing security breaches, informed users and a security-conscious workforce are also important elements of an effective cybersecurity strategy.

Cybersecurity awareness, education, training, and professional development should meet the needs of three audiences whose understanding of security issues can most benefit our preparedness as a nation: general consumers, students in primary and secondary schools and universities, and our information technology workforce. The groundwork is in place for robust educational efforts, designed for these groups through a range of programs managed through the National Initiative for Cybersecurity Education (NICE). Introduced in April 2010, NICE accords NIST responsibility for "the coordination, cooperation, focus, public engagement, technology transfer, and sustainability" of government cybersecurity education efforts. The program establishes "an operational, sustainable, and continually improving cybersecurity education program" that addresses best practices for different types of users.[97] By building on this collaborative framework, we can significantly enhance cybersecurity in America.[98]

While significant progress has been made through NICE programs that serve these target audiences, further enhancements that address the need to better-inform the general consumer are under consideration.[99] K-12, university, and advanced workforce education in cybersecurity is an important long-term investments that can bolster our nation's evolving cybersecurity posture; but our first line of defense against undiscovered vulnerabilities and fraudulent activities is in promoting the cybersecurity awareness of individual Internet users. As AT&T recommended in comments submitted in response to the NOI, consumer education programs should teach users simple, but effective, steps to keep their computers secure.[100] David Black made a point of comparison between this practical programmatic style and teaching proper auto maintenance, an activity that does not require expert knowledge of how a car works.[101]

Consistent with the need to enhance general security consciousness, many respondents' suggested that the U.S. government employ a public-

---

[97] THE WHITE HOUSE, NATIONAL INITIATIVE FOR CYBERSECURITY EDUCATION (NICE) RELATIONSHIP TO PRESIDENT'S EDUCATION AGENDA (2010), *available at* http://www.whitehouse.gov/sites/default/files/rss_viewer/cybersecurity_niceeducation.pdf.
[98] NICE has inherited all the ongoing efforts of the Comprehensive National Cybersecurity Initiative (CNCI) #8. *See* NATIONAL CYBERSECURITY INITIATIVE, *supra* note 4, at 4. Under CNCI-8 a federally focused cybersecurity education, training, awareness, and professional development initiative was established and is now being transformed into a nationally focused effort coordinated by NICE under NIST leadership of a multi agency collaboration. Currently a comprehensive strategic plan is being developed for NICE that will be ready for public review in late spring 2011.
[99] NSF and the Department of Education co-lead the formal education component of NICE.
[100] AT&T Comment at 27.
[101] David Black Comment at 3.

private joint venture to increase public awareness generally. ISACA recommended holding federal competitions like the National Cybersecurity Awareness Campaign Challenge, where individuals and groups submit ideas about how to raise awareness on a regular basis. ISACA further outlined a program that would fund contest winners with federal money, and would include universities, companies, individuals, and nonprofit groups that contribute to a national awareness strategy.[102] The original Challenge clearly captured the imagination of many and the development of a series of similar contests was widely supported in comments. DHS, which administered the Challenge, is well equipped to lead the national awareness campaign given its eight-year history of performance in this space. Subsequent "challenges" would be helpful in stimulating public awareness efforts led by the private and nonprofit sectors. For example, a new challenge could be launched to promote the development and recognition of effective educational websites suitable for different types of users – perhaps, one category for general consumers and another for technology professionals. The winning entrants would be able to use their status to distinguish themselves and increase their popularity, while furthering the cause of cybersecurity education. Other potential challenges could include developing applications that interactively guide users through the process of securing their systems, or designing web-based public service announcements as part of an ongoing awareness campaign.

In addition to raising public awareness among general consumers, we can also improve online security by promoting the creation and adoption of formal cybersecurity-oriented curricula in primary and secondary schools and universities. Respondents such as the BSA, Microsoft, and CompTIA supported a public education program in this area and recommend administering it through schools, starting in the lower grades and continuing through college.[103]

Several commenters noted that much of the private sector's focus on cybersecurity education has been to raise awareness among casual users. Commenters suggested that the government can help reduce the impact of cyberattacks by cultivating a security-conscious information technology workforce. Microsoft recommended that programming classes in universities adopt a greater emphasis on security engineering.[104] Other than individual consumers, Richard Lamb and MAAWG noted that small and medium-sized businesses are most in need of learning more about cybersecurity best practices. These businesses generally have few resources to stay abreast with cybersecurity developments; yet they

---

[102] *See, e.g.,* ISACA Comment at 6.
[103] *See, e.g.,* BSA Comment at 5; CompTIA Comment at 10; Microsoft Comment at 5.
[104] Microsoft Comment at 5.

possess sensitive data that they must protect.[105] The Federal Cyber Service, Scholarship for Service program – run by the National Science Foundation (NSF) with the support of the Office of Personnel Management (OPM), DHS, and NSA – has been effective and should continue as an effective means of training cybersecurity professionals who will find positions in the federal workforce. Additionally, NICE agencies are developing plans to increase access to information, material, best practices, and curricula that will enhance and enable the spread of good cyber hygiene and assist with the expansion and deepening of the pool of well-prepared cyber professionals. A well-trained workforce, in concert with alert consumers and educated students, can do much to advance an effective cybersecurity strategy.

(ISC)[2] raised the point that little is known about the return on investment or best practices of organizations that focus on raising awareness.[106] As NICE rolls forward, it will be important for participants to develop metrics and methods for determining return on investment. The Research Triangle Institute has developed a methodology to measure the effectiveness of cybersecurity research and has applied it to economic impact of NIST security efforts.[107] This could be a starting place to build similar measurements for other efforts.

Policy Recommendation C2:

The Department of Commerce should support improving online security by working with partners to promote the creation and adoption of formal cybersecurity-oriented curricula in schools. The Department of Commerce should also continue to increase involvement with the private sector to facilitate cybersecurity education and research.

Questions/Areas for Additional Comment:

- What new or increased efforts should the Department of Commerce undertake to facilitate cybersecurity education?
- What are the specific areas on which education and research should focus?

---

[105] *See, e.g.*, Richard Lamb Comment at 5; MAAWG Comment at 3.
[106] (ICS)[2] Comment at 4.
[107] Alan C. O'Connor & Ross J. Loomis, *2010 Economic Analysis of Role- Based Access Control*, RTI INTERNATIONAL (2010), *available at* http://csrc.nist.gov/groups/SNS/rbac/documents/20101219_RBAC2_Final_Report.pdf (report prepared for NIST).

- What is the best way to engage stakeholders in public/private partnerships that facilitate cybersecurity education and research?

3. Facilitating Research & Development for Deployable Technologies

In general, commenters agreed that academic cybersecurity research should lead to deployable technologies that address real-world problems.[108] Several commenters noted that there should be closer ties between industry and academia in cybersecurity research.[109] Commenters were divided, however, in their diagnoses of the problems as well as their proposed solutions. Some suggested giving the private sector a stronger role in setting research priorities and awarding grants,[110] while others made the case for expanding basic cybersecurity research funding.[111]

A priority-setting model that combines input from academia, industry, and government – and that drew praise from each commenter who addressed it – is the National Information Technology Research and Development (NITRD) Cyber Leap-Ahead activity.[112] In early 2009, NITRD issued a Request for Information seeking "game-changing" ideas in cybersecurity.[113] NITRD reviewed responses and grouped them into five categories. At a public summit in August 2009, industry, academia, and government gathered to review the best ideas in each category. From the summit reports, NITRD identified three initial R&D themes to exemplify and motivate future federal cybersecurity research activities: Tailored Trustworthy Spaces, Moving Target, and Cyber Economic Incentives.[114] Cyber economics – drew keen interest from several commenters on the NOI as an area to which the government should devote more resources.[115] In January 2011, DHS S&T issued a Broad Agency Announcement (BAA 11-02) on Cybersecurity Research And Development[116] that calls for research and development in fourteen Technical Topic Areas, five of

---

[108] *See* ISACA Comment at 5; (ISC)² Comment at 10; IBM Comment at 6.

[109] *See, e.g.*, Russell Thomas Comment at 16; IBM Comment at 6; Microsoft Comment at 16.

[110] *See, e.g.*, (ISC)² Comment at 10-11.

[111] *See, e.g.*, IBM Comment at 5-6; Microsoft Comment at 19.

[112] *See, e.g.*, BSA Comment at 10; U.S. Chamber of Commerce Comment at 4-5; Cisco Comment at 13; Online Trust Alliance Comment at 5.

[113] *National Cyber Leap Year Summit: Background*, NITRD.GOV, http://www.nitrd.gov/NCLYBackgroundInfo.aspx.

[114] *Federal Cybersecurity Game- change R&D: Introduction*, NITRD.GOV, http://cybersecurity.nitrd.gov/page/introduction-1.

[115] U.S. Chamber of Commerce Comment at 4-5; Cisco Comment at 13.

[116] DEP'T OF HOMELAND SEC., BAA 11-02 ,CYBER SECURITY RESEARCH AND DEVELOPMENT (2011), *available at* https://www.fbo.gov/utils/view?id=e0e9e461e907d95ea05eed74f947d3d3.

which are focused on the five categories (including cyber economics) from the August 2009 summit.

Some commenters favored even greater industry involvement in setting research priorities. For example, the MAAWG suggested that the Department of Commerce create a technical advisory board, composed of members from industry, law enforcement, and other non-academic sectors, to serve as a sounding board for the Department of Commerce as it helps set research priorities. MAAWG also recommended that board "be explicitly charged with facilitating researcher access to appropriately anonymized data from Internet operators, thereby insuring that researcher-developed models are faithful to documented reality and proposed protocols will work when deployed in the real world."[117] Another commenter pointed out that closer coordination among industry, government and academia would prevent research efforts that address problems for which commercial solutions are available.[118] The Online Trust Alliance (OTA) also sees an unmet need for funding for pilot programs, rapid prototyping, and the promotion of early adoption.[119] The government could encourage small and medium businesses participation in research by offering "fast-track" application and reporting processes.[120]

Other commenters, however, emphasized the value of keeping some distance between basic research agendas and the transfer of results into operational technologies. IBM, for example, expressed strong support for government funding for "fundamental" cybersecurity research through NSF, rather than short-term research.[121] The main issue, in IBM's view, is inadequate funding.[122] Similarly, Microsoft supported using government funding for "basic, fundamental research on the hardest problems in security," rather than development.[123]

In addition to discussing procedural routes to bring industry and academia into closer touch, commenters suggested policy steps that could give industry stronger incentives to conduct research. These included expanding the use of sole-source contracts, essentially as a way of awarding non-competitive research or development grants, though a commenter noted that this approach should be a complement to, not a

---

[117] *See, e.g.*, MAAWG Comment at 8. Note that DHS sponsors a program aimed at providing cybersecurity researchers with data collected from operational networks. *See* PREDICT.ORG, https://www.predict.org/ (last visited Mar. 28, 2011); *see also* (ISC)² Comment at 10-11.
[118] Richard Lamb Comment at 8.
[119] Online Trust Alliance Comment at 5.
[120] *Id.* at 5.
[121] *See, e.g.*, IBM Comment at 6.
[122] *Id.* at 7.
[123] Microsoft Comment at 19.

substitute for, the predominant open-call, competitively reviewed process.[124] A related idea is to have the government identify next-generation cybersecurity technologies that it would like to see broadly adopted and become the first adopter. According to Cisco, "the government could seek to order and procure a new type of product category, bearing perhaps the high cost of initial units, with spillover benefits to the private sector."[125] Research tax credits were also mentioned as a way to stimulate more private-sector cybersecurity research.[126] Along similar lines, BSA recommended that the Executive Branch and Congress create "improved IP ownership or licensing" schemes for cybersecurity research, "similar to" the Bayh-Dole Act.[127] OTA also sees an unmet need for funding for pilot programs, rapid prototyping, and the promotion of early adoption.[128] Finally, OTA noted the potential for small and medium sized businesses to do research. The government could encourage small and medium sized business participation in research by offering "fast-track" application and reporting processes.[129]

Finally, commenters pointed out broader policies that, in their views, harm cybersecurity research in academia and industry. The extent of classified research is one example. While recognizing that some classification is necessary, BSA noted that it presents a significant barrier to transferring knowledge from the government to industry.[130] IBM pointed out that one of the conditions of performing classified research – obtaining an appropriate security clearance – significantly shrinks the pool of candidates who can conduct cybersecurity research over the long term. As IBM put it, "[w]hile many of our academic institutions are the finest in the world and attract students from around the globe, after receiving their education most of them cannot get work in the cybersecurity field and leave the country with their skills or abandon the field all together."[131]

David Black also raised the more general issue of legal liability for researchers. Black urged greater legal clarity for researchers who discover software vulnerabilities and conduct penetration testing.[132] Broader legal issues, such as fear of Digital Millennium Copyright Act

---

[124] BSA Comment at 11.
[125] Cisco Comment at 16.
[126] BSA Comment at 10.
[127] *Id.* at 11.
[128] Online Trust Alliance Comment at 5.
[129] *Id.* at 5.
[130] *See, e.g.*, BSA Comment at 10.
[131] IBM Comment at 6.
[132] David Black Comment at 4.

liability or violations of communications privacy laws, did not arise in the comments.[133]

Commenters identified a wide range of topics that are, in their views, under-researched. Google stressed the importance of security usability noting that "[m]any security concerns result from UI [user interface] weaknesses rather than bad code. Too often, there is a mismatch between what the user believes she is seeing online and what is actually appearing on her screen."[134] Poor usability can hinder adoption or lead users to use secure technologies improperly, potentially undermining their value.[135] Microsoft wanted to see more research on fundamentally secure architectures and composeable trustworthy systems.[136] Other ideas included sensor device and network security, [137] code analysis tools for binaries, scripts, and source code,[138] forensics (including traceability and auditing tools),[139] and configuration management/automated configuration.[140]

Some commenters also focused on metrics, linking the paucity of good measurement to the difficulty of quantifying the economic impact of cybersecurity incidents.[141] Unreliable or poorly understood metrics can lead policy astray.[142] Other commenters stated that organizations need better ways to understand whether their security investments are effective (i.e., that they lead to better security than in the absence of those investments).[143] However, others noted that metrics are a fundamental, hard cybersecurity research problem that warrants further government support.[144] Microsoft, for example, raised the need to develop metrics that help answer questions such as "What does it mean for a product to be secure? How can one judge a product's security guarantees?"[145]

---

[133] *See* 18 U.S.C. Section 3121 specifically.
[134] Google Comment at 9.
[135] *See, e.g.,* Google Comment at 9; IBM Comment at 6; Microsoft Comment at 19-20.
[136] Microsoft Comment at 19-20.
[137] IBM Comment at 6.
[138] Microsoft Comment at 19-20 (urging an "order of magnitude improvement" in our analysis capabilities).
[139] *See, e.g.,* Honeywell Comment at 4-5; Cisco Comment at 13.
[140] Cisco Comment at 13.
[141] *See, e.g.,* Internet Security Alliance Comment at 5.
[142] *See, e.g., Id.* at 5.
[143] *See, e.g.,* Cisco Comment at 13; Internet Security Alliance Comment at 5 (suggesting that the Department coordinate empirical research into cybersecurity investment decision making and stating the need for risk mitigation metrics).
[144] *See, e.g.,* IBM Comment at 6; Microsoft Comment at 19.
[145] Microsoft Comment at 19-20. *See also* atsec Comment at 3 (discussing the need for "quality metrics" to improve design process and detect defects through sampling, rather than a "'100% inspection'").

Commenters also suggested more research into cybersecurity awareness[146] and funding for education.[147]

Commenters were generally supportive of a "grand challenge" program in cybersecurity sponsored by the U.S. government, though few had detailed comments. MAAWG suggests that the Department of Commerce and DHS partner to award an "X Prize" for "measurable objective achievements in advancing cybersecurity research."[148] Google supported the idea of a cybersecurity research grand challenge that unfolds in stages.[149] This design would allow annual progress checks, conferences, etc. in support of reaching an "ambitious but attainable" goal.[150] Microsoft, however, stated that more traditional grants awarded through the peer-review process are preferable.[151]

Policy Recommendation C3:

In cooperation with other agencies through the Federal Networking and Information Technology Research and Development (NITRD) framework, the Department of Commerce should begin to specifically promote research and development of technologies that help protect I3S from cyber threats.

Questions/Areas for Additional Comment:

- What areas of research are most crucial for the I3S? In particular, what R&D efforts could be used to help the supply chain for I3S and for small and medium-sized businesses?
- What role does the move to cloud-based services have on education and research efforts in the I3S?
- What is needed to help inform I3S in the face of a particular cyber threat? Does the I3S need its own "fire department services" to help address particular problems, respond to threats and promote prevention or do enough such bodies already exist?

---

[146] Information Use Management and Policy Institute Comment at 7.
[147] Internet Security Alliance Comment at 30 (supporting extension of programs such as Cyber Patriot to the high school level).
[148] *See, e.g.,* MAAWG Comment at 8.
[149] Google Comment at 9.
[150] *Id.* at 9.
[151] Microsoft Comment at 20.

- What role should Department of Commerce play in promoting greater R&D that would go above and beyond current efforts aimed at research, development, and standards?

D. *Ensuring Standards and Practices are Global*

The fact that cybersecurity is not defined by national borders and that the United States cannot afford to ignore global considerations was a large topic of comment on the NOI and plays a major part in how the Department of Commerce views its role in cybersecurity.

The importance of engaging with our international partners early and often on matters related to standards development and policies is an essential starting place. As indicated in comments received through the NOI, the U.S. government's engagement with foreign counterparts on the importance of using internationally accepted cybersecurity standards and practices is critical.[152] This may be the best way to achieve requisite levels of security, while preserving interoperability, openness, and economic development.

In the case of global standards development bodies (SDOs), respondents pointed to the Internet Engineering Task Force (IETF), the International Organization for Standards (ISO), and other international SDOs as venues for U.S. government participation and support for the development and adoption of global standards.

In addition to federal government representation in SDOs, commenters urge the Department of Commerce and U.S. government to remain involved in other international forums concerned with cybersecurity. For example, TechAmerica asks that the U.S. government be sure to engage the private sector in the development of policy positions and partnership programs in these multinational, regional and bilateral forums "in order to develop and cultivate norms for behavior that support greater global cybersecurity."[153]

A number of respondents, notably TechAmerica supported by (ISC)², went beyond advocating the use of existing engagement methods and recommended establishment of an Ambassador for cybersecurity at the State Department[154] to coordinate international engagement and

---

[152] ITI Comment at 3-6.
[153] TechAmerica Comment at 22.
[154] Subsequent to the Cybersecurity NOI comment period, the State Department announced the creation of the first Coordinator for Cyber Issues in an effort to more

strategy.[155] MAAWG asks the Department of Commerce to "consider establishing its own specialized, technical 'boots on the ground' abroad, staffed by career employees with specialized cyber knowledge and expertise."[156]

Several comments urged the United States to lead by example.[157] Respondents recommend against any attempt by the U.S. government to unilaterally develop cybersecurity standards that could contradict or confuse other standards used internationally.[158] Atsec and others argue instead for the United States to help develop and promote adoption of international standards, both domestically and overseas.[159]

A few respondents mentioned the need for capacity building. Cisco advised that the United States should substantially increase its technical assistance programs, noting that education about the benefits of global standards, interoperability, and security is critical. Because security threats can originate anywhere in the world, nations facing the most acute challenges should also be given the most support.[160] IBM advocates assisting developing countries in adoption of international standards, rather than enabling these nations to create barriers to market entry.[161] MAAWG went further stating that many countries that have the greatest need for enhanced cybersecurity also require reference materials in native languages.[162]

Respondents also supported the use of internationally accepted "cybersecurity principles" in the area of standards and conformity assessment procedures. ITI qualified that principles would be useful depending on the forum and format they take and requested that should such an effort be taken, that it include robust consultation with industry at the outset.[163] Atsec indicated that "[a]greement on a simple set of 'cybersecurity principles' would do much to guide the development and implementation of current and future norms" as well as help reduce the risks of introducing trade barriers.[164]

---

effectively advance U.S. foreign policy interests abroad. See: http://www.state.gov/r/pa/prs/ps/2011/04/161485.htm.

[155] *See, e.g.*, TechAmerica Comment at 21; (ISC)² at 8.

[156] MAAWG Comment at 7.

[157] *See, e.g.*, atsec Comment at 5-6; Honeywell Comment at 5; (ISC)² Comment at 10; ITI Comment at 3.

[158] *See, e.g.*, atsec Comment at 5; (ISC)² Comment at 10; ITI Comment at 3.

[159] atsec Comment at 5.

[160] Cisco Comment at 11.

[161] IBM Comment at 5.

[162] MAAWG Comment at 4.

[163] ITI Comment at 7-8.

[164] atsec Comment at 6.

Policy Recommendation D1:

The U.S. government should continue and increase its international collaboration and cooperation activities to promote cybersecurity policies and standards, research and other efforts that are consistent with and/or influence and improve global norms and practices.

Questions/Areas for Additional Comment:

- Are there additional ways in which the Department of Commerce can work with other federal agencies and stakeholders to better cooperate, coordinate, and promote the adoption and development of cybersecurity standards and policy internationally?

IV. Conclusion

The Task Force offers these policy recommendations to establish a more secure Internet environment.

Consistent with the wide range of policies outlined in the Administration's *International Strategy for Cyberspace*[165] and leveraging the dispersed knowledge and wisdom of the American people, our continued engagement with all stakeholders is critical to enhancing our national cybersecurity posture. Accordingly, the Department of Commerce's Task Force is seeking further comment on the issues enumerated in this report and how current cybersecurity activities can be improved to serve consumer interests, innovation, and national economic goals. The Department intends for the comments responding to this green paper to contribute to the Administration's domestic policy and international engagement in the area of cybersecurity.

---

[165] THE WHITE HOUSE, INTERNATIONAL STRATEGY FOR CYBERSPACE (2011) available at http://www.whitehouse.gov/sites/default/files/rss_viewer/international_strategy_for_cyberspace.pdf.

Appendix A: Summary of Recommendations and Questions for Further Discussion

Recommended Definition of Internet and Information Innovation Sector (I3S):

The Department of Commerce should designate a new sector, called the Internet and Information Innovation Sector (I3S), to capture functions and services that fall outside the classification of covered critical infrastructure and have a large potential for growth, entrepreneurship, and vitalization of the economy. More specifically, the following functions and services are included in the I3S:

- provision of information services and content;
- facilitation of the wide variety of transactional services available through the Internet as an intermediary;
- storage and hosting of publicly accessible content; and
- support of users' access to content or transaction activities, including, but not limited to application, browser, social network , and search providers.

Questions/Areas for Additional Comment:

- How should the Internet and Information Innovation Sector be defined? What kinds of entities should be included or excluded? How can its functions and services be clearly distinguished from critical infrastructure?
- Is Commerce's focus on an Internet and Information Innovation Sector the right one to target the most serious cybersecurity threats to the Nation's economic and social well-being related to non-critical infrastructure?
- What are the most serious cybersecurity threats facing the I3S as currently defined?
- Are there other sectors not considered critical infrastructure where similar approaches might be appropriate?
- Should I3S companies that also offer functions and services to covered critical infrastructure be treated differently than other members of the I3S?

Policy Recommendation A1:

The Department of Commerce should convene and facilitate members of the I3S to develop voluntary codes of conduct. Where subsectors (such as those with a large number of small businesses) lack the resources to establish their own codes of conduct, NIST may develop guidelines to help aid in bridging that gap. Additionally, the U.S. government should work internationally to advance codes of conduct in ways that are consistent with and/or influence and improve global norms and practices.

Questions/Areas for Additional Comment:

- Are there existing codes of conduct that the I3S can utilize that adequately address these issues?
- Are there existing overarching security principles on which to base codes of conduct?
- What is the best way to solicit and incorporate the views of small and medium businesses into the process to develop codes?
- What is the best way to solicit and incorporate the views of consumers and civil society?
- How should the U.S. government work internationally to advance codes of conduct in ways that are consistent with and/or influence and improve global norms and practices?

Policy Recommendation A2:

The Department of Commerce should work with other government, private sector, and non-government organizations to proactively promote keystone standards and practices.

Questions/Areas for Additional Comment:

- Are the standards, practices, and guidelines indicated in section III. A. 2 and detailed in Appendix B of the Green Paper appropriate to consider as keystone efforts? Are there others not listed here that should be included?
- Is there a level of consensus today around all or any of these guidelines, practices and standards as having the ability to improve security? If not, is it possible to achieve consensus? If so, how?
- What process should the Department of Commerce use to work with industry and other stakeholders to identify best practices, guidelines, and standards in the future?

- Should efforts be taken to better promote and/or support the adoption of these standards, practices, and guidelines?
- In what way should these standards, practices, and guidelines be promoted and through what mechanisms?
- What incentives are there to ensure that standards are robust? What incentives are there to ensure that best practices and standards, once adopted, are updated in the light of changing threats and new business models?
- Should the government play an active role in promoting these standards, practices, and guidelines? If so, in which areas should the government play more of a leading role? What should this role be?

Policy Recommendation A3:

The U.S. government should promote and accelerate both public and private sector efforts to research, develop and implement automated security and compliance.

Questions/Areas for Additional Comment:

- How can automated security be improved?
- What areas of research in automation should be prioritized and why?
- How can the Department of Commerce, working with its partners, better promote automated sharing of threat and related signature information with the I3S?
- Are there other examples of automated security that should be promoted?

Policy Recommendation A4:

The Department of Commerce, in concert with other agencies and the private sector, should work to improve and augment conformance-based assurance models for their IT systems.

Questions/Areas for Additional Comment:

- What conformance-based assurance programs, in government or the private sector need to be harmonized?

- In a fast changing and evolving security threat environment, how can security efforts be determined to be relevant and effective? What are the best means to review procedural improvements to security assurance and compliance for capability to pace with technological changes that impact the I3S and other sectors?

Policy Recommendation B1:

The Department of Commerce and industry should continue to explore and identify incentives to encourage I3S to adopt voluntary cybersecurity best practices.

Questions/Areas for Additional Comment:
- What are the right incentives to gain adoption of best practices? What are the right incentives to ensure that the voluntary codes of conduct that develop from best practices are sufficiently robust? What are the right incentives to ensure that codes of conduct, once introduced, are updated promptly to address evolving threats and other changes in the security environment?
- How can the Department of Commerce or other government agencies encourage I3S subsectors to build appropriate best practices?
- How can liability structures and insurance be used as incentives to protect the I3S?
- What other market tools are available to encourage cybersecurity best practices?
- Should federal procurement play any role in creating incentives for the I3S? If so, how? If not, why not?

Policy Recommendation B2a:

Congress should enact into law a commercial data security breach framework for electronic records that includes notification provisions, encourages companies to implement strict data security protocols, and allows states to build upon the framework in defined ways. The legislation should track the effective protections that have emerged from state security breach notification laws and policies.

Policy Recommendation B2b:

The Department of Commerce should urge the I3S to voluntarily disclose their cybersecurity plans where such disclosure can be used as a means to increase accountability, and where disclosure of those plans are not already required.

Questions/Areas for Additional Comment:

- How important is the role of disclosure of security practices in protecting the I3S? Will it have a significant financial or operational impact?
- Should an entity's customers, patients, clients, etc. receive information regarding the entity's compliance with certain standards and codes of conduct?
- Would it be more appropriate for some types of companies within the I3S be required to create security plans and disclose them to a government agency or to the public? If so, should such disclosure be limited to where I3S services or functions impact certain areas of the covered critical infrastructure?

Policy Recommendation B3:

The Department of Commerce should work with other agencies, organizations, and other relevant entities of the I3S to build and/or improve upon existing public-private partnerships that can help promote information sharing.

Questions/Areas for Additional Comment:

- What role can the Department of Commerce play in promoting public-private partnerships?
- How can public-private partnerships be used to foster better incentives within the I3S?
- How can existing public-private partnerships be improved?
- What are the barriers to information sharing between the I3S and government agencies with cybersecurity authorities and among I3S entities? How can they be overcome?
- Do current liability structures create a disincentive to participate in information sharing or other best practice efforts?

Policy Recommendation C1:

The Department of Commerce should work across government and with the private sector to build a stronger understanding (at both the firm and at the macro-economic level) of the costs of cyber threats and the benefits of greater security to the I3S.

Questions/Areas for Additional Comment:

- What is the best means to promote research on cost/benefit analyses for I3S security?
- Are there any examples of new research on cost/benefit analyses of I3S security? In particular, has any of this research significantly changed the understanding of cybersecurity and cybersecurity related decision-making?
- What information is needed to build better cost/benefit analyses?

Policy Recommendation C2:

The Department of Commerce should support improving online security by working with partners to promote the creation and adoption of formal cybersecurity-oriented curricula in schools. The Department of Commerce should also continue to increase involvement with the private sector to facilitate cybersecurity education and research.

Questions/Areas for Additional Comment:

- What new or increased efforts should the Department of Commerce undertake to facilitate cybersecurity education?
- What are the specific areas on which education and research should focus?
- What is the best way to engage stakeholders in public/private partnerships that facilitate cybersecurity education and research?

Policy Recommendation C3:
Through its continued research efforts, the Department of Commerce should begin to specifically promote research and development of technologies that help protect I3S from cyber threats.

Questions/Areas for Additional Comment:

- What areas of research are most crucial for the I3S? In particular, what R&D efforts could be used to help the supply chain for I3S and for small and medium-sized businesses?

- What role does the move to cloud-based services have on education and research efforts in the I3S?
- What is needed to help inform I3S in the face of a particular cyber threat? Does the I3S need its own "fire department services" to help address particular problems, respond to threats and promote prevention or do enough such bodies already exist?
- What role should Department of Commerce play in promoting greater R&D that would go above and beyond current efforts aimed at research, development, and standards?

Policy Recommendation D1:

The U.S. government should continue and increase its international collaboration and cooperation activities to promote cybersecurity policies and standards, research and other efforts that are consistent with and/or influence and improve global norms and practices.

Questions/Areas for Additional Comment:

- How can the Department of Commerce work with other federal agencies to better cooperate, coordinate, and promote adoption and development of cybersecurity standards and policy internationally?

Appendix B: Widely Recognized Security Standards and Practices

This Green Paper discusses developing "codes of conduct." We see these codes as essentially utilizing technical standards (which we refer to simply as "standards"), procedures to implement a specific policy ("practices") and recommended sets of controls and standards ("guidelines") under a set of high level aspirational policy goals ("principles") and performance measures.

There are numerous approaches available today that are widely recognized as important standards and practices that either are or could be utilized broadly by industry as baselines to build these codes of conduct. While many of these standards and/or practices are often targeted towards particular sectors or entities, many still are widely applicable beyond their intended targets and often provide far-reaching guidelines and/or baselines for cyber-security. Outlined below are several such examples:

Payment Card Industry Data Security Standard (PCI DSS)

The PCI DSS is a standard defined by the Payment Card Industry Security Standards Council, developed to help organizations proactively protect sensitive customer account data. PCI DSS is a multifaceted security standard that includes requirements for security management, policies, procedures, network architecture, software design and other critical protective measures.[166] PCI DSS compliance is governed by industry self-regulation. Individual payment brands have their own compliance enforcement practices, including financial or operational consequences to certain businesses that are not compliant.

Summary of Implementation Status:

All merchants that accept payment cards are required to comply with PCI DSS. Global payment brands – American Express, Discover Financial Services, JCB International, MasterCard Worldwide, and Visa Inc. – incorporate the PCI DSS as technical requirements for their data security compliance programs, which applies to entities that hold, process, or exchange cardholder information from cards branded with logos of the card brands.

---

[166] For more detailed information, see:
https://www.pcisecuritystandards.org/security_standards/index.php.

Benefits:

Even for those companies that do not participate, the PCI DSS offers a set of baseline security standards and practices for protecting sensitive information.

- Increase customer trust;
- Protect data;
- Prevent credit card fraud; and
- Prevent other security threats

Challenges:

- Meeting the technical requirements of standard is achievable, but educating employees on the proper handling of cardholder data is another factor that has proven difficult;
- Perception that a minimal baseline of security is not enough;
- Perception that the PCI DSS requirements are too expensive to implement; confusing to comply with, or subjective in their interpretation and enforcement; and
- Some NOI commenters felt that the standard provides excellent advice, but may require more time and resources not available to small businesses and entrepreneurs that may act as a barrier to entry for small and medium sized businesses.[167]

NIST SP 800-53

As stated in the Federal Information Security Management Act (FISMA), NIST is responsible for developing security standards (Federal Information Processing Standards – FIPS) and guidelines (Special Publications (SP)) applicable to federal systems. The SPs in the 800 series present documents of general interest to the computer security community.[168] Of particular note is SP 800-53 Recommended Security Controls for Federal Information Systems. These guidelines apply to all components of information systems that process, store, or transmit federal information. While developed to help achieve more secure information systems within the federal government, SP 800-53 is often utilized by non-federal government and commercial organizations.

Summary of Implementation Status:

As stated above, SP 800-53 was developed as a set of recommended security control guidelines applicable to federal information systems. A

---

[167] *See, e.g.,* MAAWG Comment at 3; CompTIA Comment at 3.
[168] A complete listing of Special Publications in the 800 series is available at: http://csrc.nist.gov/publications/PubsSPs.html.

subsequent NIST standard (FIPS 200[169]) made SP 800-53 a requirement for unclassified federal information systems and agencies were required to comply with SP 800-53 within a year of FIPS 200 publication, date of March 9, 2006.[170]

Benefits:

The NIST SP 800 series, and SP 800-53 in particular:

- Helps public and private sectors establish baseline security practices responsive to ever-changing technologies and risks;
- Provides stable, yet flexible catalog of security controls for information systems to meet current organizational protection needs and the demands of future protection needs based on changing requirements and technologies; and
- Creates a foundation for the development of assessment methods and procedures for determining security control effectiveness.

Challenges:

- The revision process for SP 800-53 is too static to keep up with quickly emerging threats and/or protection technologies;
- SP 800-53 is too flexible and overly complex and as such requires a deep knowledge of controls in order to utilize it effectively in a variety of situations; and
- Low and moderate impact systems (covered by SP 800-53) are often no longer relevant in a world of increasingly high-end threats and that all systems need to be protected against the types of attacks or attackers associated with high impact systems.

Identity Management & Authentication and the National Strategy for Trusted Identities in Cyberspace (NSTIC)

A significant number of respondents urged the Task Force to promote more widespread use of state-of-the-art authentication and ID management systems to reduce the incidents of successful cyber intrusions and attacks. Others, while not disparaging the need for better authentication and ID management, urged the Task Force to recognize that identity solutions do not solve every cybersecurity issue and could serve to make the Internet less private and secure if implemented poorly.

---

[169] NATIONAL INSTITUTE OF STANDARDS AND TECHNOLOGY, MINIMUM SECURITY REQUIREMENTS FOR FEDERAL INFORMATION & INFORMATION SYSTEMS (2006), *available at* http://csrc.nist.gov/publications/fips/fips200/FIPS-200-final-march.pdf.
[170] *Id.* at 5.

There are many existing examples of improved authentication and security, from one-time passwords to token-based solutions. These technologies can be built at different levels of development and utilization. When used independently, these technologies mitigate particular online vulnerabilities and are generally most effective when broadly deployed and utilized. When layered, technology solutions such as these have the potential to greatly enhance security and could contribute to an effective identity management architecture based on authentication. Yet, these solutions have had trouble gaining traction in the marketplace because of a variety of concerns outlined in the comments received during the NOI including liability, privacy and usability.[171]

In addition, on April 15, 2011, President Obama issued the NSTIC, calling for action to address these concerns. NSTIC will help establish identity solutions and privacy-enhancing technologies to help improve the security and convenience of sensitive online transactions. These solutions and technologies will help improve processes for authenticating individuals, organizations, and underlying infrastructure – such as routers and servers. NSTIC was developed with substantial input from the private sector and the public and it will be led by the private sector, in partnership with the federal government, consumer advocacy organizations, privacy experts, and others.

The NSTIC calls for the development of interoperable technology standards and policies – the Identity Ecosystem – that improves upon the passwords currently used to login online. The Identity Ecosystem will provide people with a variety of more secure and privacy-enhancing ways to access online services. The Identity Ecosystem enables people to validate their identities securely when they are doing sensitive transactions (like banking) and lets them stay anonymous when they are not (like blogging). The Identity Ecosystem will enhance individuals' privacy by minimizing the information they must disclose to authenticate themselves.

NSTIC's Identity Ecosystem is a vibrant marketplace that provides people with choices among multiple identity providers – both private and public – and choices among multiple credentials. For example, a student could get a digital credential from her cell phone provider and another one from her university and use either of them to login to her bank, her e-mail, her social networking site, and so on, all without having to remember dozens of passwords. People and institutions could have more trust online because all participating service providers will have

---

[171] *See, e.g.*, MAAWG at 6.

agreed to consistent standards and practices for identification, authentication, security, and privacy.

As directed by the President, the Department of Commerce intends to establish a National Program Office (NPO) that will be led by NIST, with activities involving public policy and privacy protections in the commercial sector to be led by NTIA. The NPO will coordinate the federal activities needed to implement NSTIC. The office would be the point of contact to bring the public and private sectors together to meet this challenge.

Benefits:

Like other solutions suggested in this Appendix, NSTIC will not solve every security issue, but by fully implementing NSTIC and developing the Identity Ecosystem it describes, what could help:

- Limit unauthorized transactions, and decrease the transmission of identifying information resulting in less risk from data breaches and identity theft;
- Provide a platform on which new or more efficient and secure business models (including in sectors such as health and financial);
- Display and protect their brands online. Participants in the Identity Ecosystem also will be more trusted, because they will have agreed to the Identity Ecosystem's minimum standards and practices for privacy and security; and
- Make attribution easier in certain cases of cybercrime.

Challenges:

The private sector-led partnership called for in the NSTIC must overcome barriers in the current environment that inhibit the adoption of more trustworthy identities in cyberspace. Such barriers include:
- Concerns regarding personal privacy;
- Lack of secure, convenient, user-friendly options for authentication and identification;
- Uncertainty regarding the allocation and level of liability for fraud or other failures; and
- The absence of a common framework to help establish trusted identities across a diverse land-scape of online transactions and constituents.

Internet Protocol Security (IPSEC)

The Internet Protocol (IP) has enormous flexibility in the use of packets. Each packet contains data that is small, easily handled and maintained. However, with the advantages of IP come disadvantages. The routing of these packets through the Internet as well as other large networks makes them open to security risks such as spoofing, sniffing, and session hijacking.

IPSEC is a security protocol suite that provides cryptographically based data authentication, integrity, and confidentiality as data (at the IP packet level) is transferred between communication points across IP networks. [172] IPSEC is designed to protect both the Internet Protocol version 4 (IPv4) and the updated version 6 (IPv6). [173] IPSEC emerged as a viable network security standard because enterprises wanted to ensure that data could be securely transmitted over the Internet.

Implementation Status:

IPSEC was developed in conjunction with the most current version of the Internet Protocol - IPv6 and is therefore "built-in" to all standards-compliant implementations of IPv6. While developed after the previous version of the Internet Protocol – IPV4, IPSEC is designed to protect IPv4 as an optional protocol extension. Despite this, due to the slow deployment of IPv6, IPSEC is most commonly used today in securing IPv4 traffic.

Benefits:

The benefits of implementing and using IPSEC are:

- Provides security directly on the IP network layer and secures everything put on top of the IP network layer;
- Relatively mature protocol that has proven to be a secure and trusted method of securing data;
- Transparent to applications in the sense that IPSEC is not limited to specific applications; and
- Transparent to end users and therefore no need to train users on security mechanisms.

---

[172] S. Kent & K. Seo, *Security Architecture for the Internet Protocol*, INTERNET ENGINEERING TASK FORCE REQUEST FOR COMMENT 4301(2005), *available at* http://tools.ietf.org/html/rfc4301.
[173] Currently, the Internet is largely based on IPv4, but due to the exhaust of IPv4 address space, organizations and countries are moving to adopt/deploy IPv6, which offers a vast amount of addresses.

Challenges:

- IPSEC has a great number of features and options, making it very complex. This complexity increases the likeliness of weaknesses or holes being discovered; and
- Limitations to implementing in a Network Address Translation (NAT) environment.

Domain Name System Security

The Domain Name System (DNS) is a critical component of the Internet infrastructure that is used by almost every Internet protocol-based application to associate human readable computer hostnames with the numerical addresses required to deliver information on the Internet. The accuracy, integrity, and availability of the information supplied by the DNS are essential to the operation of any system, service, or application that uses the Internet. The DNS was not originally designed with strong security mechanisms to ensure the integrity and authenticity of the DNS data. Over the years, a number of vulnerabilities have been identified in the DNS protocol that threaten the accuracy and integrity of the DNS data and undermine the trustworthiness of the system.

To mitigate vulnerabilities in the DNS, the Internet Engineering Task Force (IETF) developed a set of protocol extensions to protect the Internet from certain DNS related attacks: DNSSEC. DNSSEC is designed to address man-in-the-middle attacks and cache poisoning by authenticating the origin of DNS data and verifying its integrity while moving across the Internet. DNSSEC protects against forged DNS data by using public key cryptography to digitally sign DNS data when it comes into the system and then validate it at its destination. Digital signing helps assure users that the data originated from the stated source and that it was not modified in transit.

Implementation Status:

The root of the DNS was signed July 2010, which contributed to significant deployment of DNSSEC among Top Level Domains (TLDs). As of February 2011, 66 TLDs were signed. While this is significant compared to the handful of signed TLDs prior to July 2010, it still represents only a fraction of the 306 TLDs in the root zone. On a positive note, the largest TLDs have or are in the process of signing their zones. Commercial ISPs, such as Comcast, are beginning to offer DNSSEC validation. Due in large part to NIST and DHS efforts, great strides have been made with respect to DNSSEC implementation in federal systems. FISMA required DNSSEC to be implemented in .gov sites by December

2009. The .gov root is now signed and full DNSSEC deployment across .gov is underway.

Despite this progress in deployment, DNSSEC is not yet widely known or deployed according to Forrester research commissioned by VeriSign. [174] Among the 297 global IT decision makers surveyed, some 57 percent of respondents had never heard of DNSSEC. Overall, only 11 percent have deployed DNSSEC. However, among those who know DNSSEC, 95 percent indicated they either have already deployed or have plans to deploy.

Benefits:

- DNSSEC that is broadly deployed and utilized will have the effect of providing additional security by preventing man-in-the-middle attacks and cache poisoning; and
- Effectively deployed and utilized, DNSSEC will provide the above protection to domains, websites, and email;

Challenges:

- DNSSEC is a sound solution to a specific Internet vulnerability within the DNS, but it must be complemented by other layers of security;
- Broad implementation of DNSSEC introduces a set of complex changes that impact the entire Internet ecosystem and requires extensive resources, documentation, testing, and industry coordination; and
- DNSSEC is most effective when universally implemented. This level of implementation is still in its infancy and will require concerted and cooperative effort as well as time to reach full potential.

Internet Routing Security

The core routing of the Internet is done through a protocol called Border Gateway Protocol (BGP), which makes it possible for ISPs to connect to each other and for end-users to connect to more than one ISP. Like many early Internet protocols, BGP was not developed with security in mind. Thus, there are many known BGP vulnerabilities including accidental failures and malicious attacks. The propagation of false routing information in the Internet can deny service to small or large portions of the Internet as well as lead to cascade failures, which can have enormous implications for users.

---

[174] Forrester Consulting, Research Study, *DNSSEC Ready For Prime Time* (2010), *available at* http://www.verisigninc.com/assets/dnssec-ready-for-prime-time-by-forrester-research.pdf.

The IETF, with support and participation from DHS and NIST, has working groups looking at the issue of BGP security. This includes Secure BGP (S-BGP or BGPSEC), soBGP, PGBGP, etc. Securing the routing system with authentication solutions such as these would require enterprises to operate a certificate authority function (use of certificates) so they can digitally sign and certify that they own a particular IP address block and have the authority to sub-delegate it, outsource it, or make some other decisions about how its traffic is routed.

Implementation Status:

Several proposed solutions to BGP security have been developed over the years, but none has been universally adopted. While a comprehensive approach to BGP security has not yet been settled, NIST has developed a set of best practices that can help in protecting BGP (SP 800-54).[175]

Benefits:

- More secure/authenticated BGP would benefit operators, and users of the Internet.

Challenges:
- Lack of consensus and motivation to derive common and widely deployable standard techniques to mitigate the problems;
- Any solution to routing issues is likely to require substantial effort, cost, and time to deploy; and
- The perception that these and other authentication mechanisms are complex and difficult to implement/operate.

Web Security

Web applications and the transactions that take place over them are central to the success of the Internet. Secure Sockets Layer (SSL) is a protocol that establishes a secure session link between a user's web browser and a website. All communications transmitted through this link are private and secured using encryption. SSL uses digital certificates to encrypt data exchanges between a user and a website, thereby protecting the confidentiality of financial transactions, communications, e-commerce, and other sensitive interactions.

---

[175] National Institute of Standards and Technology, Border Gateway Protocol Security 6 (2007), *available at* http://csrc.nist.gov/publications/nistpubs/800-54/SP800-54.pdf.

To enable SSL on a website, a SSL certificate needs to be acquired from a certificate authority[176] and installed on the website's server. The use of an SSL certificate on a website is usually indicated by a padlock icon in web browsers. When a SSL certificate is installed on a website, a visitor to that website can be sure that the information entered there is secured and only seen by the organization that owns the website. SSL uses digital certificates to validate the identity of a website. When those certificates are issued by reputable third-party certificate authorities (CAs), SSL assures users of the identity of the website owner. However, SSL does not ensure that a user reaches the intended site, so it is not applicable against attacks that redirect users. In other words, SSL site validation is effective, but only if a user reaches the correct destination first.

Implementation Status:

Several versions of the protocol are in widespread use in applications such as web browsing and e-mail, and arguably is the most widely deployed security protocol used today. It is embedded in all popular browsers and engages automatically when the user connects to a web server that is SSL-enabled, which is visible to users as *https.* The "s" indicates a secure connection.

Benefits:

- SSL secures communications between a user's web browser and website;
- Designed to be transparent to higher level protocols; and
- Requires little interaction from the end user when establishing a secure session – a simple experience for the end user.

Challenges:

- Costs are involved for SSL providers to set up trusted infrastructure and validate identities;
- Performance and latency can be an issue for websites with very large number of visitors; and
- End user understanding and expectation of SSL is limited.

Email Security

Email is another widely used and relied upon application that would benefit from authentication. Email authentication assists in the battle against spam, but also works to ensure that legitimate/authentic emails get passed the spam filters. Efforts to date have largely focused on two

---

[176] A "certificate authority" is an entity that issues digital certificates to organizations or people after validating them.

ways in which to authenticate emails – sender authentication and content authentication.

Sender authentication mechanisms focus on the "sender" and are designed to protect against forgery of email sender identities, either in the envelope or in the header. Examples of this are Sender Policy Framework (SPF) and Sender ID. Both protocols use path registration by mapping the IP address to the domain name. The identity being authenticated through these mechanisms is the operator of an access system rather than the content author or their organization.

Content authentication mechanisms aren't concerned with the *sender* like SPF and SenderID, but instead authenticate the author of the message *content* through asymmetric cryptographic methods. DomainKeys Identified Email (DKIM) is somewhat of a hybrid of sender authentication and content authentication as it ties the authenticity of the message content to the message's alleged sender identity. That is, in order for a message to be regarded as valid, its signature must be successfully verified as well as the sender domain in the message header.

Implementation Status:

A number of prominent email service providers are implementing and or support email authentication mechanisms.

Benefits:

- These solutions offer effective tools in the campaign against spam and phishers; and
- New implementations offer demonstration in email reader that the email is from a specific sender aiding consumer education.

Challenges:

- Email authentication does not solve spam or ensure security. Like most security solutions, they need to be layered with other solutions to ensure the most comprehensive approach to security;
- DKIM's cryptographic components involve overhead and complexity; and
- Most email authentication mechanisms have difficulties handling email forwarding.

Appendix C: Acknowledgements

The Internet Policy Task Force extends its thanks to all of the individuals and private sector organizations who participated in our public Symposium on Cybersecurity in the Commercial Space, and those who submitted written comments to the Notice of Inquiry that served as the basis for this report.

Symposium panelists

Ruben Barrales, President and CEO of the San Diego Regional Chamber of Commerce

Michael Barrett, Chief Information Security Officer, PayPal

Vint Cerf, Vice President, Google

Larry Clinton, President, Internet Security Alliance

Michael Deer, Director of Privacy, Sears Holdings Corporation

Mischel Kwon, Vice President of Public Sector Security Solutions, RSA

Kristin Lovejoy, Vice President of Security Strategy, IBM

Mark Mattis, Director of Information Security, Compliance, and Infrastructure Support, Costco Wholesale Corporation

Cheri McGuire, Director of Critical Infrastructure & Cybersecurity, Microsoft (now Symantec)

Joe Pasqua, Vice President of Research, Symantec

Don Proctor, Senior Vice President for Cybersecurity, Cisco Systems

Philip Reitinger, Deputy Under Secretary of the National Protection and Programs Directorate, Department of Homeland Security

Dan Schutzer, Executive Director, Financial Services Technology Consortium

Ken Silva, Chief Technology Officer, VeriSign

Murray Walton, Senior Vice President and Chief Risk Officer, Fiserv, Inc.

Lee Warren, Chief Information Security Officer, United Technologies Corp.

Notice of Inquiry Respondents

American National Standards Institute
atsec
AT&T
BITS
Black, David
Business Software Alliance
Center for Democracy and Technology
Cisco Systems
CompTIA
CTIA
Cyber Risk Partners
Cyveillance, Inc.
Document Orchards
Google
Honeywell Int.
IBM
Information Technology Industry Council
Information Use Management and Policy Institute
Institute for National Security and Counterterrorism
Internet Security Alliance
ISACA
(ISC)2
Lamb, Richard
Messaging Anti-Abuse Working Group
Microsoft Corporation
National Business Coalition on E-Commerce and Privacy
Network Solutions
Online Trust Alliance

.ORG Public Interest Registry

PayPal

Secure ID Coalition

Smart Card Alliance

StopBadware

Synaptic Laboratories Limited

TechAmerica

Technology Assurance Alliance

Thomas, Russell C.

Tigers Lair

Triad Biometrics

University Bank

USTelecom

U.S. Chamber of Commerce

U.S. Council for International Business

VeriSign

Vertical Horizons One

Wave Systems

We would also like to thank the Commerce staff without whom this Green Paper would not have been possible. In particular, Marc Berejka and Ari Schwartz deserve special mention for leading this project. Curt Barker, Jon Boyens, Ashley Heineman, and Alfred Lee were invaluable in their efforts as well. In addition, we also would like to thank our many colleagues the Executive and Legislative branches who have provided valuable feedback and consultation during the development of this report.

We offer special thanks to the President's Cybersecurity Coordinator Howard A. Schmidt for his efforts to develop sound policies.

www.ingramcontent.com/pod-product-compliance
Lightning Source LLC
Chambersburg PA
CBHW060501060326
40689CB00020B/4603